THE PLAY OF THE UNMENTIONABLE

THE PLAY OF THE UNMENTIONABLE

AN INSTALLATION BY JOSEPH KOSUTH
AT THE BROOKLYN MUSEUM

ESSAY BY DAVID FREEDBERG
INTRODUCTION BY CHARLOTTA KOTIK

WITH 126 ILLUSTRATIONS,
21 COLOUR, 105 DUOTONE

THAMES AND HUDSON

…the history, and not just in terms of ethnology, of sexual prohibitions:
to speak of the constantly shifting and obstinate forms of repression in our own culture,
and not to write a chronicle of morality or of tolerance, but to
reveal how the limits of the Western world and the origins of its morality are its
tragic division from the happy world and from desire.

MICHAEL FOUCAULT

ACKNOWLEDGEMENTS

'The Brooklyn Museum: The Play of the Unmentionable,' and this book,
benefited greatly from the generous help of Wolfgang Berkowski,
Ted Byfield, Tim Daly Screenprinting, Exhibition Techniques, Paul Lammertink,
Anne Livet, Carol Mangan, Jill McArthur, Doreen McCarthy, Max Moerman,
Dan Reynolds, Lincoln Tobier, Jon Tower, Alice Weatherford,
Blair Wrinkle, and Martin Zimmerman.

TABLE OF CONTENTS

PREFACE

Robert T. Buck

The series of projects begun in the Grand Lobby of The Brooklyn Museum in 1984 has given artists a unique opportunity to explore their ideas on a truly grand scale, and frequently to create pieces that would not otherwise have been conceived. Encompassing works by painters, sculptors, and installation artists alike, the series has helped renew interest in environmental or site-specific works.

Joseph Kosuth's was the twenty-fourth project in the Grand Lobby series, and it proved to be one of the most memorable for both the museum and the artist. From the beginning of his career, Kosuth—like many other conceptual artists—has produced work that is more widely recognized in Europe than in the United States. Although he has had more than a hundred one-man exhibitions in galleries and museums since the late 1960s, "The Brooklyn Museum Collection: The Play of the Unmentionable" was his first solo exhibition in any museum in New York City.

Kosuth's installation was mounted at a time of concentrated attack on the National Endowment for the Arts, a federal organization that for the past twenty years has served the arts in this country with a foresight and dedication unmatched by any of the well-funded government art agencies of Western Europe, and with progressive policies that have brought Americans to the forefront of the international art scene. The Brooklyn Museum has been a recipient of numerous grants in various categories and for many exhibitions, and thus we all rallied behind a project that took up the cause of the NEA and the principles of creative freedom it represents.

"The Play of the Unmentionable" was drawn exclusively from the museum's collections. All the exhibited works were at one point or another deemed controversial. Everyone working on the project found a fine sort of irony in the fact that, with this exhibition, we demonstrated that museums across the land are filled with objects that would never pass the funding criteria discussed presently in Congress.

In these times of raging controversy, the museum's curators and administrators pondered Kosuth's proposal carefully, weighing their responsibility toward the institution against the potential impact of the installation. Ultimately the proposal won unanimous approval, and, with a feeling of utmost urgency, the entire staff eagerly cooperated. The goal was to participate in a project designed to protect our freedom of expression—the very essence of American spirit and the exact freedom for which so many have come to these shores, abandoning loved ones and material possessions. "The Play of the Unmentionable" was named as the most important exhibition of 1991 by the Frederick B. Weissman Art Foundation, which awarded both the artist and the curator special prizes; it was also the winner of the Municipal Arts Society's Certificate of Merit.

Developed over the summer of 1990, the project required the attention of practically everyone in the museum. I would like to take this opportunity to thank all the staff members whose expertise and dedication made "The Play of the Unmentionable" such a success: in the department of Contemporary Art, Charlotta Kotik, who selected Joseph Kosuth and, together with Brooke Kamin Rapaport and Laura Deer Moore, organized the project; in African, Oceanic, and New World Art, Diana Fane and William Siegmann; in Asian Art, Amy Poster, Layla Diba, and Xiaoping Lin; in Decorative Arts, Kevin Stayton, Barry Harwood, and Marianne Loggia; in Egyptian, Classical, and Middle Eastern Art, Richard Fazzini, James Romano, Donald Spanel, and Robert Biancchi; in Painting and Sculpture, Linda Ferber, Barbara Gallati, Teresa A. Carbone, Sarah Faunce, and Elizabeth Easton; in Prints and Drawings, Linda Kramer and Karyn Zieve; in Conservation, Ken Moser, Ellen Pearlstein, and Carolyn Tomkiewicz; in Collections Management, Cathryn Anders; in Design, Daniel Weidmann, Jeffrey Strean, and Michael Rizzo; in Editorial, Elaine Koss and John Antonides; in Marketing, Rena Zurofsky; in Photography, Patricia Bazelon and Patty Wallace; in the Art Reference Library, Deirdre Lawrence; in the Archives, Deborah Wythe; in Public Information, Sally Williams and Michelle Menendez; in Government and Community Relations, Patricia Falk; and in the Administrative Offices, Roy Eddey, Linda Ferber, and Larry Clark.

The public responded to "The Play of the Unmentionable" with incredible interest and overwhelming approval. Visitors streamed to the museum and membership soared. What at first seemed a potential danger to the institution proved to be one of the most popular exhibitions in years. It has been a learning experience not only about art but about history and politics as well. The Brooklyn Museum enjoys a most diverse audience, both ethnically and economically. And much like the jurors in Cincinnati who supported Dennis Barrie's decision to exhibit Robert Mapplethorpe's photographs, these members of the general public all spoke clearly in favor of the creative process and the American freedoms of expression and choice in all walks of life.

ROBERT T. BUCK
DIRECTOR
THE BROOKLYN MUSEUM

INTRODUCTION

Charlotta Kotik

When I proposed late in 1988 that Joseph Kosuth be considered for one of The Brooklyn Museum's Grand Lobby projects, I naturally foresaw that he would produce a work of great intellectual complexity. I was far from envisioning, however, the richness of the project he would propose. In the Grand Lobby series, as in all installation projects, the artist's freedom holds primacy. This means that the curator relinquishes much of his or her usual curatorial power, and becomes instead a collaborator and a facilitator of the artist's plans. Sharing in the direction of the project leads to a fusion of the more traditional roles of artist and curator and makes the Grand Lobby installation process a unique experience.

Joseph Kosuth's installation "Zero & Not" at the Leo Castelli Gallery had once again turned my attention to the work of this most ardent of the original proponents of Conceptual Art. Kosuth's continued commitment to an aesthetics

that elevated the idea above the aura of an object was liberating, especially after nearly a decade of relentless art-world exploration of traditional forms resulting primarily in a surfeit of marketable objects. But it was not only his recent work that led to my consideration of Joseph Kosuth for the Grand Lobby. His work, and that of other conceptual artists, had always held a special fascination for me. Those of us who came of age in the late 1960s in what was then termed Eastern Europe and were interested in contemporary art had to rely on information in magazines and books often brought secretly into the country. Art that had not been officially approved or heavily censored was considered extremely dangerous to the stability of the reigning systems. For that reason, Walter Benjamin's famous treatise "The Work of Art in the Age of Mechanical Reproduction" took on special meaning for students behind the Iron Curtain:

mechanical reproduction and the printed word were frequently the only routes to a fragmented knowledge of contemporary art, aesthetics, philosophy, and politics. The world was reduced to the two-dimensional narrative of printed signs. Therefore, work that in its conception relied on photographic and literal descriptions of objects, such as Kosuth's "One and Three Chairs" of 1965, was easier to decipher, to comprehend, and to remember. Another aspect of conceptualism that made it a revered movement for many of my generation was its questioning of the institutions of painting and sculpture, and of the status quo in general. The subversive character of conceptual works was directed not only against the art establishment, but against all establishments, thus aligning itself with the goals of a younger generation striving for liberation from an oppressive social order.

My fascination with Kosuth's work grew when he turned to major twentieth-century thinkers for inspiration. In 1981 he began a series of works that stressed the pervasive yet frequently ambiguous influence of Sigmund Freud's ideas on modern social thought. In "Word, Sentence, Paragraph," from the series "Zero & Not," a segment of Freud's text was reproduced but rendered almost illegible by a line of white neon running through the words. In this case, that which obscured also illuminated. In the project preceding The Brooklyn Museum's, "The Play of the Unsayable: Wittgenstein and the Art of the Twentieth Century," organized for the Vienna Secession and the Palais de Beaux-Arts, Brussels, Kosuth paid homage to the Viennese philosopher Ludwig Wittgenstein, whose centennial the exhibition celebrated. In that installation, works by numerous artists were displayed along with Wittgenstein texts, silkscreened on the walls and grouped to demonstrate the role of language in art. Kosuth's positioning of these texts within and between the works of art highlighted Wittgenstein's perspective on the future of philosophy and aesthetics. In these groupings, Wittgenstein's original concept was shifted and new meanings were established.

The proposal Kosuth submitted to The Brooklyn Museum in the summer of 1990 applied this strategy of juxtaposition and recontextualization to the right-wing political ideas that endanger society's freedoms. For that purpose, he enlisted the supposedly apolitical disciplines of art history, archaeology, and ethnography in an unlikely alliance. Each was invoked to illuminate not only whole stylistic epochs and particular works of art, but also our constantly changing perception of historical periods and individual masterpieces. Kosuth demonstrated that just as the relationships within society constantly evolve, so does our comprehension and judgment of artworks and cultural artifacts.

In keeping with his concerns of the past twenty years, Kosuth's new project sidestepped the traditionally defined aesthetic criterion of what constitutes an artist's "work." Using the collection of The Brooklyn Museum as a kind of readymade, Kosuth created an installation that played with the traditional curated exhibition. In his opinion, an artist's activity consists not simply in fashioning objects but in making meaning; so while this exhibition served to address an issue of current concern, he saw the installation itself as a legitimate part of his activity as an artist. The works presented—more than a hundred—ranged from an Egyptian stone relief of 1300 B.C. to a recent work by Barbara Kruger, from a Kashmir sculpture of the eighth century to four bronzes by Auguste Rodin done at the turn of this century, and from engraved seventeenth-century English glassware to Marcel Breuer's Bauhaus armchair. Of equal weight within this installation of "borrowed" works were enlarged texts, some contemporary and some older, some propagandistic and some theoretical, framing and reframing the viewer's perspective. These texts commented on and were commented on by the surrounding artworks. Taken together, they led the viewer to consider and question the meaning of cultural production. Whether we will be permitted to see such a range of work in the future, Kosuth seemed to say, is brought into question by the assault on art going on in the United States today.

"The Brooklyn Museum Collection: The Play of the Unmentionable" presented works accorded the idealized concept of timeless, classical beauty next to works tending toward a dizzying urgency of the moment. Because the objects were drawn from the collection of an encyclopedic museum, the installation reflected not only the history of art but also the history of taste—in other words, how the perception of cultural artifacts changes according to time and place. The museum is a privileged depository of objects and ideas from the past, and it is a mandate of the museum to collect broadly, to care properly for its collections, and to conduct ongoing research into the origins and meaning of every object in order to ensure their proper preservation and presentation. The interpretation of the work is of utmost importance: it furthers and deepens our knowledge of our own heritage, thus allowing us to understand ourselves and our contemporaries better. But it is this very interpretation that is most ideologically charged, and that changes most dramatically in reaction to social shifts in a constantly evolving society. The struggle among the proponents of various interpretations is a natural and positive development as long as it does not stifle the freedom of expression of one or all—the greatest injustice a society can bestow on itself. By juxtaposing works from diverse cultures and times with one another and with diverse texts, "The Brooklyn Museum Collection: The Play of the Unmentionable" encouraged a dialogue growing from comparisons and based on one artist's unique vision.

In an artist's statement accompanying the exhibition, Kosuth wrote:

> It would be very difficult for me to do an exhibition in an American public institution supported by funds from the National Endowment for the Arts without responding to the present attack on artists, cultural institutions, and the NEA itself by the radical Right. I have, as well, a personal relationship to this issue. Around 1970 I was called by Brian O'Dougherty, who was then in charge of the Visual Arts Division at the NEA. He told me that the endowment had been receiving applications from artists with the words 'Painting' and 'Sculpture' crossed off and the words 'Conceptual Art' written in. Since he suggested that I was at least partly responsible for this situation, he asked me if I would help him out and come to Washington as a consultant for the selection process. After agonizing for some time whether I wanted to be a government employee—even for one day—I decided that I'd better do it; if I didn't, a lot of work that very much needed support might not get it.
>
> There were applications from all over the country. It was fascinating to see the diverse, nontraditional activities of artists in places like Florida and Idaho, as well as by peers of mine in New York. I remember trying most to give grants to those artists who would have the least chance of getting support from the art market. I felt

then, as I feel now, that supporting such artists is really the whole point of the NEA. If artistic activity is totally dependent on the tastes of the art market it will suffer in a way that will have serious long-term repercussions. It would be as if all scientific and medical research were limited to what pharmaceutical companies decided would make them money that year. The grant-giving institutions of the federal government have, understandably, great flexibility in following the advice of their experts and specialists in research in science. Why should they behave any differently with regard to art?

One objective of "The Brooklyn Museum Collection: The Play of the Unmentionable" is to show that, while no one has problems with the authority works now represent as 'masterpieces,' the cultural power that so legitimizes them flows directly from the provocative nature of the history of ideas as experienced through the lives of real men and women. Beyond any individual's opinion of what 'obscene' may be, it is the responsibility of this society not just to protect, but also to nourish, the conditions within which the free flow of ideas will flourish. In many ways art history is the residue, the record, of these human conditions. As a process itself, art protects as it empowers the right to self-expression. Its history is the history of the capacity of all our freedoms to put consciousness to form, and thereby manifest their self-perception. Protecting this consciousness that art produced is an important part of the protection of our political liberty.

When Kosuth outlined his idea for an installation with the theme of the censorship of art as exemplified in various cultures and ages, curators from The Brooklyn Museum's departments of African, Oceanic, and New World Art, American Painting and Sculpture, Asian Art, Decorative Arts, Egyptian, Classical, and Middle Eastern Art, European Painting and Sculpture, and

Prints and Drawings began a series of meetings to discuss the feasibility of the proposal. Although every staff member agreed with the need to respond to the threat raised against the freedom of artistic expression by the radical Right, not everyone saw the potential of doing so by using the varied collection of this old and encyclopedic museum. In such an institution, every object has a special place, and there was a shared concern that the intrusion of the artist-turned-curator could harm the traditional perception of the objects by taking them out of context. There are restrictions inherent in the highly specialized training of various disciplines that, when translated into museum practice, results in rules that are hard to change. For the individual curators, opening the field to an outsider who might harm the integrity of the collections as well as the individual objects was a difficult decision to make, and quite contrary to any established museum practice. But the urgency of the main theme—the defense of creative freedom—prevailed, and the curators devoted countless hours to sifting through their records to identify works that were once considered controversial by the powers that be. Historical shifts in perception were coming to light, and the reasons for the changes—usually power struggles within political or religious systems—were fascinating.

The artist hired Max Moerman, a graduate student of religious studies from Stanford University, to be his assistant and the liaison to the museum. Moerman worked closely with the curators on selecting and organizing the objects into several distinct categories according to Kosuth's instructions. The curators searched for works with accepted artistic merit, not merely those pieces that happened to serve the project's purposes. The exhibition was essentially grouped around the female and male nude, the presentation of the child as nude, religious and political controversies, and questions of propriety in artistic representation. Unexpected configurations and comparisons emerged, such as those between a photograph by Robert Mapplethorpe and a male nude by Auguste Rodin, between iconoclasm in ancient Egypt and iconoclasm in medieval Europe, and between the latent eroticism of an early twentieth-century society portrait of a semiclad child and the openly sexual images of Larry Clark's portfolio *Teenage Lust*.

Many works had to be taken from their permanent place of installation in the museum. Rather than replacing them with other pieces, notices were posted in their former locations pointing to their incorporation in the temporary installation in the Grand Lobby. This practical measure tied the spaces of the museum into one conceptual unit, and helped to strengthen the integrity of the installation. Not all the objects selected were masterpieces. Lesser-known or infrequently exhibited works were displayed next to those currently considered among the museum's most valued, providing all involved with a new look at the collection, revealing the special characteristics of individual works, and demon-

strating changing tastes. The salonlike display style was modified in this case by a nonhierarchical approach to the positioning of works, and by the placement of large areas of silkscreened text next to the objects. Although there was a lot of text—Kosuth's wall text as well as identifying labels prepared by the departmental curators—the installation was not didactic. Visitors were encouraged to move freely among the groups of objects and to contemplate each piece independently.

There was much to be learned from this unusual display, which shed light on the sociopolitical changes in different societies as represented in their extant works of art. But to see the museum filled with virtually thousands of people every day, some casual museum-goers and some artists, art historians, and other professionals, was the greatest reward to all of us entrusted with the preservation of our cultural heritage. It was, in the face of the assaults on culture from the Right, a strong affirmation of the important role of museums in today's society.

CHARLOTTA KOTIK
CURATOR OF CONTEMPORARY ART
THE BROOKLYN MUSEUM

THE INSTALLATION

INSTALLATION PHOTOGRAPHS BY KEN SCHLES

The mode of iconoclasm which is called censorship does not necessarily take the form of direct assault or removal. Its cunning consists in denying its own operation and leaving no scars.

LEO STEINBERG,
The Sexuality of Christ in Renaissance Art
and in Modern Oblivion

WILLEM DE KOONING
(AMERICAN, B. 1904)
Woman, 1953–54
OIL ON PAPER, 57.124
GIFT OF MR. AND MRS. ALASTAIR BRADLEY MARTIN

"I found pictures at the exhibition that are simply lewd and others that are lewd only to artists."

MILTON BROWN,
The Story of the Armory Show

One should add that the natives' response to th...
recorded, provides evidence of a comparable r...
ished at the French custom of collecting...
handkerchiefs, wryly declared: "If thou likest...
chief and I will soon fill it."

The savage lives within himself, while social man
stantly outside himself and only knows how to l
opinion of others, so that he seems to receive the co
of his own existence merely from the judgment
concerning him.

JEAN JACQUES R

The artist does not create for the artist: he creates for the people and we will see to it that henceforth the people will be called in to judge its art.

ADOLF HITLER

The people who assail images do so in order to make clear that they are not afraid of them, and thereby prove their fear. It is not simply fear of what is represented; it is fear of the object itself.

DAVID FREEDBERG, *The Power of Images*

NEW KINGDOM, DYNASTY XVIII, REIGN OF AKHENATEN
EGYPT; FROM HERMOPOLIS, BUT ORIGINALLY FROM AKHETATEN, MODERN AMARNA
(CIRCA 1352–1336 B.C.)
Nefertiti, Chief Queen of Akhenaten, Kissing Her Daughter Merit-Aten
LIMESTONE, 60.197.8
CHARLES EDWIN WILBOUR FUND

THOMAS EAKINS
(AMERICAN, 1844–1916)
William Rush Carving His Allegorical Figure of the Schuykill River, 1908
OIL ON CANVAS, 39.461
DICK S. RAMSAY FUND

Sooner or later we shall have to get down to the humble task of exploring the depths of our consciousness and dragging to the light what sincere bits of reflected experience we can find. These bits will not always be beautiful, they will not always be pleasing, but they will be genuine.

EDWARD SAPIR,
"CULTURE, GENUINE AND SPURIOUS"

CINDY SHERMAN
(AMERICAN, B. 1954)
Untitled, 1985
COLOR PHOTOGRAPH, 86.36
FRANK L. BABBOTT FUND AND CHARLES S. SMITH MEMORIAL FUND

When the makers of Pepsi Cola moved into the Thai soft drink market, they began an advertising campaign with the American slogan, 'Come alive, you're in the Pepsi generation'. The company said it later realized that the Thai translation it was using said, 'Pepsi brings your ancestors back from the dead'.

THE NEW YORK TIMES

If left unchecked, we and perhaps other nations like us will continue to sell the technology which produces visual symbolic forms, while at the same time teaching other peoples our sort only, our conceptions, our codes, our mythic and narrative forms. We will, with technology, enforce our notions of what is, what is important, and what is right. The questions that anthropologists have been struggling with (related to whether we as anthropologists should help the oppressed as well as the oppressor), whether we should take sides in questions of culture change or even culture description, assume new dimensions when transformed from physical to symbolic forms. While answers are not simple in this area, should we not consider the question whether we who strive to learn about others should take some responsibility for helping others to learn about themselves? Should we not consider whether we have a responsibility, at the very least, to explain to those we study that new technologies of communication need not be used only in the ways of the technological societies that introduce them?

Sol Worth, *STUDYING VISUAL COMMUNICATION, POLITICS OF SYMBOLISM*

new of what constitutes the
... in a culture which also hold
... her in Biblical or in parch
... who believe that other col-
... g so their own categorie
... int our own unexamined co
... always see them as striving
... ms to me that, when we a
... the good, for granted, othe
... ntaining "potment" rather
... t.

Carpenter (1971) reports in *TV Guide* that his own introduction of pictures in 1970 to people in New Guinea created
vast changes in a short time. He reports that after the taking
of pictures of a circumcision ritual, the people gave up the
ritual and substituted pictures for it.

Sol Worth, *STUDYING VISUAL COMMUNICATION, POLITICS OF SYMBOLISM*

the sanguine and terrifying aspects of primitive life, which
civilized individuals could hardly sustain, precisely because
of the immediate personal-genesis in which they occur, do
not begin to compete with the mass, impersonal, rationalized
slaughter that increases in scope as civilization spreads and
deepens. . . . Certain ritual dramas or aspects of them
acknowledge, express, and symbolize the most destructive,
ambivalent, and demonstrable aspects of human nature; in so
doing, they are left liminal and finite; that is, they become
self-limiting. For this, as yet, we have no civilized parallel,
no functional equivalent.

Stanley Diamond, *IN SEARCH OF THE PRIMITIVE*

PAUL GAUGUIN
(FRENCH, 1848–1903)
Tahitian Woman, CIRCA 1891
PASTEL ON PAPER, 21.125
MUSEUM COLLECTION FUND

AUGUSTE RODIN
(FRENCH, 1840–1917)
Damned Women, 1885–1911, CAST 1979
BRONZE, 86.87.4
GIFT OF B. GERALD CANTOR ART FOUNDATION

Their patterns of political, economic, and artistic behavior were forgotten—even the languages they had spoken in Africa. Like the poor whites of the South, they gathered together instead for fervent Christian revivalist camp meetings: they sang the hymns the poor whites sang, and if they sang them better and invented countless variations of great poignancy, nevertheless the old forms which they had achieved in Africa were forgotten. Conditions of slavery in America were so drastic that this loss is not to be wondered at. The slaves in any one plantation had come from tribes speaking mutually unintelligible languages, and with mutually unfamiliar arts of life; they had been herded together like cattle in slave ships and sold at the block in a strange and frightening world. They were worked hard on the plantations. It is no wonder that their owners remarked on their lack of any cultural achievements; the mistake they made was to interpret the degradation of the slave trade as if it were an innate and all-time characteristic of the American Negro. The Negro race has proud cultural achievements; not for very good reasons they were not spread before our eyes in America.

RUTH BENEDICT, *Race: Science and Politics*

THOMAS HOVENDEN
(AMERICAN, 1840–1895)
Ain't That Ripe?, CIRCA. ?
OIL ON CANVAS, 32.825
GIFT OF THE EXECUTORS OF THE ESTATE OF COLONEL MICHAEL FRIEDSAM

DESIGNED BY KARL L. H. MÜLLER
(AMERICAN, B. GERMANY, 1820–1877)
Tête-a-tête Tea Service, 1876
MADE BY THE UNION PORCELAIN WORKS (1863–CIRCA 1922)
HARD PASTE PORCELAIN, 68.87.28-32
GIFT OF FRANKLIN CHACE

CHELSEA PORCELAIN MANUFACTORY
(LONDON, ENGLAND, 1745–1784)
America and Europe, 1758–1759
PORCELAIN, 50.12.54
BEQUEST OF JAMES HAZEN HYDE

PHILIP EVERGOOD
(AMERICAN, 1901–1973)
The Tooters, 1961
OIL ON CANVAS, 62.76
GIFT OF THE FORD FOUNDATION

EGYPT, SAID TO BE FROM ALEXANDRIA
(PTOLEMAIC PERIOD, 305–30 B.C.)
Symplegma OR *A Group of Intertwined Figures*
LIMESTONE, 58.13
CHARLES EDWIN WILBOUR MEMORIAL FUND

INDIA, PROVINCIAL MUGHAL, OUDH
Intoxicated Ascetics, CIRCA 1775
OPAQUE WATERCOLOR AND GOLD ON PAPER, 84.183
ANONYMOUS GIFT

RS:

You created "The Play of the Unmentionable," the current show at The Brooklyn Museum, which illustrates history's changing views of art and obscenity. How did this project come about?

JK:

Two years ago, I was asked by Charlotta Kotik, the museum's curator of contemporary art, if I would be willing to do an exhibit for the museum's Grand Lobby series. I've lived in New York most of my life, and, although I've had many one-man shows in museums and galleries around the world, I've never had a museum show here. So I was very happy to be asked to do something. They began looking around for funding, and last spring I was told that the National Endowment for the Arts, among other groups, had agreed to support the exhibition. The more I considered the idea of accepting funds from the NEA, the more I felt I wanted to do something that would respond to the current assault on art and artists.

RS:

All of the objects in the show—over a hundred—come from the museum's own collection. Is there a reason for that?

JK:

In terms of its holdings, The Brooklyn Museum is a cross between the Metropolitan Museum of Art and the Smithsonian Institution; many of the cultural artifacts here were originally used by its predecessor, the Brooklyn Institute, as parts of another kind of exhibit, one more ethnographic and scientific than "artistic" in its emphasis. I was trying to think of some way to use these things that was both continuous with the main body of my work, which is concerned with problems of interpretation and epistemology, and that would also raise the level of debate in the current controversy. It occurred to me that the collection here was full of works—both "art" and other kinds of objects—that had one connotation in their original context and a completely different one today; and I realized that this fact could be used to provide a comment on how people's response to art tends to be determined by the "frame," social or political or cultural, in which they tend to see it. And that, of course, is the underlying issue in the present debate.

RS:

The exhibit ranges from conventionally recognized masterworks to some sexually explicit contemporary works. Have you had any complaints?

JK:

That possibility is itself a very important aspect of the show. Works that eventually come to be seen as masterpieces, and that thereby reflect a certain cultural authority, do so precisely because they represented serious problems for their original audiences. Now, however, most of the work in the show has been stamped with an official seal of approval. The paintings by Matisse and Picasso and Braque are ones that every good Republican would love to hang in his dining room, but children were prohibited from seeing them when they appeared here in the 1913 Armory show, because they were thought to be somehow morally subversive. Most of the office furniture in midtown Manhattan derives from the designs of the Bauhaus group, but it was considered such a threat to cultural decency when it came out that the Nazis had to close it down.

RS:

You describe yourself not as the "curator" of this exhibit but as its "creator." What exactly is it that you've created here?

JK:

If art is to be more than expensive decoration, you have to see it as expressing other kinds of philosophical and political meaning. And that varies according to the context in which you experience it. This particular exhibit tries to show that artworks, in that sense, are like words: while each individual word has its own integrity, you can put them together to create very different paragraphs. And it's that paragraph I claim authorship of.

RS:

Most of your other work has been concerned with fairly rarefied issues of art-world theory. Why, with this show, have you embraced a more explicitly polemical set of concerns?

JK:

When political might gets behind a campaign steeped in ignorance and intolerance, it's time for everyone to become concerned. I always took a certain amount of pride in the simple fact that we have an NEA, and that the agency is able to spend government funds in support of diverse activities that are not immediately pragmatic. It's the equivalent of pure research in science; imagine all of our scientific and medical research being directed by pharmaceutical companies, and you'll have a pretty good idea of what the art world would be like without the NEA. It seems to me that part of the responsibility of a society is to nurture the conditions in which a free flow of ideas can occur, and art is part of that.

RS:

What sort of response have you had from audiences?

JK:

Some people appear to be shocked that such things could ever appear in a museum. They tend to see a museum as an oasis away from the problems of the world; but my art has always tried to resist a position in which we're supposed to be passive consumers of culture—here it is, this is what it means. I refuse to do that. The viewers complete the work. They're the other half of the making of meaning.

RS:

You also maintain a home and a studio in Belgium. What do Europeans think about America's current debate over the NEA?

JK:

Europeans see themselves as the guardians of civilization. They are amused and fascinated—but not altogether surprised—by many of the stories they hear about the United States. And the idea that there are some crackpot senators who have a myopic view of culture—and who have, in some ways, actually succeeded in affecting the conversation of serious people—is absolutely hilarious to them. What's the fuss? They've been looking at stuff like this in museums all their lives.

RS:

The show includes several wall quotes from Hitler's *Mein Kampf,* reflecting Nazi attitudes toward "degenerate" art, and they are clearly meant as a comment on the current political situation here. Isn't that a rather harsh comparison to make?

JK:

I've found people to be surprised and disturbed by them. We've reduced the Nazi period to a set of images and sound bites in popular culture, and I wanted to remind viewers that there was a very specific mentality that preceded Nazi domination and made it possible. When we see the success that the radical Right has had with this issue, we have to remember that this is really the beginning of a kind of evil. And voices must be raised.

THIS INTERVIEW WAS ORIGINALLY PUBLISHED BY *New York Newsday,* OCTOBER 15, 1990, AND IS REPRINTED WITH THE PERMISSION OF RANDALL SHORT AND *New York Newsday.*

JOSEPH KOSUTH AND THE PLAY OF THE UNMENTIONABLE

David Freedberg

There is, of course, a tell-tale sign: as if to warn against the possibility of any erotic thought that she might arouse, a small cross hangs beside the left thigh of Hiram Powers's *Greek Slave* (p. 73). And while she certainly covers herself modestly with her right hand (it is the same gesture of modesty as the ancient statues known as the *Venus Pudica*), the heavy chain that binds her hands and gives a further clue to the intended subject of the sculpture seems to act as nothing so much as some kind of ancient chastity belt. Not surprising, we might think, that this smooth and perfect form should have been one of the great artistic successes of the Universal Exhibition at the Crystal Palace in London in 1851; but surely not only because of the chaste thoughts she aroused in her beholders? The very idea of an impure thought, however, would have been swiftly denied by the sculptor—

31

whether by repression or rationalization, though, we cannot really know. After all, he had a clear moral view of the subject, apparently inspired by accounts of how, during the Greek war of independence of 1821–1830, the Turks took a number of beautiful Greek girls as prisoners in order to sell them on the slave market. "These were Christian women," he wrote,

> and it is not difficult to imagine the distress and even despair of the sufferers while exposed to be sold to the highest bidders. *But as there should be a moral* in every work of art, I have given to the expression of the Greek Slave what trust there could still be in a Divine Providence for a future state of existence, with utter despair for the present, mingled with somewhat of scorn for all around her.

We may suppose that not everyone would have troubled so long with the expression of the *Greek Slave*—at least not long enough to discern this moral. For even then she must have seemed, were it not for the sign of the cross, more pagan Venus than Christian slave. And can the artist himself have been unaware of the most famous story associated with the ancient statue of Venus that served as the direct artistic model for his work, the *Venus of Cnidos*? For, as Pliny, Lucian, Aelian, and many others recount, this was the statue that so excited a young man of Cnidos that one night he stole out of town in order to be alone with her, and left on her beautiful form the very evidence of his desire.

But one does not, of course, have this sort of thought inside a museum, let alone a museum that began with as much a scientific as an artistic purpose, and where the moral dimension was so pronounced. Or does one? In the same year as the Universal Exhibition, the Brooklyn Institute—the precursor of The Brooklyn Museum—received $12,000 in order to endow a series of Sunday Night Lectures on "The Power, Wisdom and Goodness of God as Manifested in His Works"; and a few years later, its large collection of casts of Greek and Roman sculptures was especially singled out by a group of clergymen as providing evidence of the noblest qualities of Man. These may not be the first things that come to mind as we look at the Roman statues of Dionysos and Apollo in the context of the objects displayed alongside them in Joseph Kosuth's "The Play of the Unmentionable" (pp. 88–93); instead, the texts and objects Kosuth has assembled for this installation force us to ask ourselves about their meaning both to ourselves and to others, and to be honest about those meanings. They also make us face these inevitable questions: In what ways are the puritanisms of the mid-nineteenth and late twentieth centuries different from each other? What are the implications of such differences? And what effect do our concepts of art—of what art is, or should be—have on judgments of this kind?

The Brooklyn Museum started as a "museum of everything" (as former director, Thomas S. Buechner, once put it). It was meant to cover the world: by no means only a museum of art, it was also a museum of science and ethnography. The objects it held ranged from an entire Hindu street to the best collection in the world of kachina dolls, as well as stuffed bears and fifty-five thousand dried butterflies. As soon as the new cultural institution was on a secure footing, a huge palace of a museum was commissioned from the noted New York architects of McKim, Mead & White, to be constructed in their best classical style. To the burghers and patrons of Brooklyn, no style could have seemed more appropriate for the housing of art and for the architectural declaration of its public status. Although the building may now seem grand enough, only *one sixth* of the original plan was constructed. By 1934 the decision had been taken to restrict the range of the great museum to art and ethnography alone (by then, of course, ethnography had become institutionalized and naturalized as art). Natural History was abolished. The taxidermists took their leave, and one of them expressed his fears for the future in these words: "Modern art was beginning to show its ugly, incomprehensible forms with a vengeance, and there would be no place for anything else, so I decided to look for another job."

Art replaced science, and an old anxiety was again awakened, though not for the first time—that the radical and the unpalatable might become institutionalized as art. In fact, 1934 was the year in which McKim, Mead & White's monumental entrance staircase was removed. This was done in the interests of modernism: not only would the entrance appear more in keeping with the modern spirit, the museum would seem (it was supposed) more accessible to the people.

No nexus could have been more fragile than that one, of modern art and its public. In 1933, for example, the Nazi SS wrote a letter to Mies van der Rohe in Berlin concerning the recently closed Bauhaus. (This institution, probably more than any other, was responsible for the change of taste that dictated the removal of the grand staircase in faraway Brooklyn.) The SS letter declared that the Bauhaus could only be reopened on the following conditions: Vassily Kandinsky and Ludwig Hilberseimer were to be fired, the curriculum was to be changed in accordance with the dictates of the Ministry of Culture, and the faculty was to sign its full agreement with the new conditions.

That such a letter was in perfect tune with Hitler's views on art is made clear by Kosuth's characteristically challenging mosaic of quotations. "Challenging" because Kosuth constantly makes us revise views we take altogether for granted, and he makes us reflect on positions that we unthinkingly accept. For example, although it is hard to imagine agreeing with any utterance of Hitler's—let alone with the sentiment behind it—

Kosuth confronts us with at least one view of his that, *on the face of it*, seems quite laudably democratic: when it comes to art, the people are the judge. But beware of taking the view out of context. Soon the material Kosuth presents makes us realize, or remember, that things are never so simple. What Hitler means is that the artist must submit his will to "the sure and healthy instinct of the people." The transcendent, God-given artist is, above all, *decent*; he must eschew all radicalism, and must not paint blue meadows and green skies. If he does so because this is the way he feels or experiences things, he is either defective or a liar. Accordingly, there is to be no painting for small cliques; the artist must produce an art that can, from the outset, count on the readiest and most intimate agreement of the great mass of the people (whose instincts, clearly, are more reliable than those of the artists). Otherwise it is a matter for the criminal court.

There is no great distance between clusters of views such as these and the ones expressed at the time of the Chicago Armory Show of 1913. The works of the Cubist artists, like those of Matisse, were regarded either as forms of mystification, charlatanry, insanity, or simply as hoaxes. At best, such artists were believed to be guilty of insincerity. Their pictures corrupted public morals—especially, of course, the morals of children and women (notoriously more susceptible than men). M. Blair Coan, the inspector for the Senatorial Vice Commission declared that Futurist art was immoral, and that every girl in Chicago was being given the opportunity of *gazing* (not just looking) at examples of distorted art. When a clergyman saw the art on display, he had to turn back his flock of children at the head of the stairs, lest they see the latest degeneracies from Paris. A schoolteacher denounced the exhibition as nasty, lewd, and immoral, while his superintendent declared it off-limits. The Chicago Law and Order League called for the suppression of the exhibition altogether.

35

Who would have thought that views like these could return with such vengeance in 1990? One had believed them to be dead and buried. But no: the guardians of public morality—and others whom one might have thought less concerned about the well-being of ordinary men and women —revived the old connections between art (above all modern art) and immorality. They did so in order to wave the banner of corruption, degeneracy, and the decline not just of morality, but of society as a whole. The two things—corruption of art and corruption of society—obviously go together. Although it is true that the issues seemed the same as they always had been, there was one significant difference. Having assimilated—however uncomfortably, however meagerly—some of the realities of female sexuality, society was able, in 1990, to be less inclined to hide its general fear of sexual representation behind fears for the corruption of women. But now there was some new threat to deal with (or, to put it more accurately, some threat that was newly out in the open): the representation of homosexuality. Naturally, the anxieties about children and sexuality remained. Once again the great social fears were acted out in the domain of art.

The year 1990 saw the trial of the Cincinnati Contemporary Arts Center and its director Dennis Barrie, the Reverend Donald Wildmon's legal pursuit of David Wojnarowicz, the National Endowment for the Arts' rejections, equivocations, and volte-faces over the performances of Karen Finley and Holly Hughes. Already in 1989 one could detect the beginning of a kind of general hysteria about the permissible and the unmentionable gripping not only the radical Right but also both houses of Congress and a largely craven public press. From every quarter came renewed pressure for the government to control and legislate the arts. Puritanism, prudishness, and hostility to homosexuality—all as usual in the guise of preserving the best and purest of civilization from degeneracy and corruption—had waited in the wings. Now they could return to center stage. The prosecution of the Cincinnati arts center and Barrie for "pandering obscenity" and for "the illegal use of children in nudity-related material" by having publicly exhibited seven photographs by Robert Mapplethorpe swiftly became the most famous of these episodes. Proceedings began on September 24 and concluded on October 5. This is the background to "The Play of the Unmentionable," and it is in this context that it had—and has—to be seen. The installation opened at The Brooklyn Museum on September 26, the day before the selection of the jury at the trial in Cincinnati.

Asked by The Brooklyn Museum to produce one of the installations for which he was already famous, Kosuth knew that financial support would at least partly have to come from the National Endowment for the Arts. But since he is an artist especially well known for his critiques of the institutionalization of art, the subject of the installation, in 1990, must have seemed both inevitable and urgent. It was to examine the consequences of the institutionalization of art for artistic liberty. His installation would be both a reflection and a provocation. Its aim would be to engender self-reflexiveness in each viewer's judgment about the relations between art, morality, and censorship. It was to be less overtly theoretical than his previous installations such as those at the Freud Museum (1982) and in commemoration of the Wittgenstein centennial in Vienna and Brussels (1989), and more specifically related to current political issues. But the theoretical *armature* of the Brooklyn installation was closely linked to the earlier ones, and the view of the nature of artistic work and the place of the installation within it remained the same. It was the logical outcome of Kosuth's long engagement with the problems of the production of meaning, with the role of context in the making of both art and meaning, and with the dialectical relations between viewer and work of art.

The Vienna-Brussels installation, "Wittgenstein: The Play of the Unsayable," was predicated on the second of the agendas in the great philosopher's *Tractatus Logico-Philosophicus*: to demonstrate that what could not be spoken was necessarily to be left unsaid, or to be omitted. (This was clearly different from the first of his agendas, which was to give an articulate basis for what *could* be said). Kosuth's aim was to suggest the ways in which meaning was produced through the *play* of what was not or could not be said. He did so by using both artworks and texts, juxtaposed in such a way as to elicit self-consciousness about context (both personal and institutional) and about the way in which one's notion of art depended on context. At this stage in Kosuth's thought, the idea was that art provides the evidence for what cannot be said, or for what can be said only indirectly. If art can never *say* anything directly, it has the power of being able to *show* that which cannot be said.

For over twenty-five years Kosuth has been producing mosaiclike juxtapositions in such a way as to produce new (or surplus) meanings that go beyond the individual texts and objects made by others. These mosaics of appropriated texts and objects become works in their own right, in which new meanings arise in the interstices between texts and texts, texts and objects, objects and objects. The Brooklyn installation was thus a work like any other by Kosuth. Fundamental to everything that he has done is the belief that meaning cannot reside in the object or the text alone and is in no sense autonomous. The meaning of a work of art depends wholly on its context and on its relations with the viewer. Meaning, as Wittgenstein himself declared, lies in use. If the Wittgenstein show was about the unsayable, the Brooklyn installation was about that still more remote category, the unmentionable. If art is able to show, even to describe, that which cannot be said, it is even more capable of showing that which cannot be mentioned. The point of the Brooklyn installation was to enable, through the play of these unmentionables, the laying bare of what we are no longer allowed to mention (because of the coils of institutionality), or cannot bring ourselves to mention (because of repression). This Kosuth achieved by juxtaposing objects selected from The Brooklyn Museum's collection, and by displaying texts around them on the walls of the Grand Lobby (and now collected in this volume). In making his selection from the museum, and in explicitly acknowledging the subvention from the NEA, Kosuth was able to raise a whole series of questions in the minds of his viewers, beginning with these: What is the role of the institution in the formation of our view of art? Who, finally, decides what is art and what is not art? What are the consequences of that decision? How do our own views of art affect our moral judgments about representation and, therefore, our larger moral and political judgments?

The choice may seem to lie between acceptance of the rules and fetishization on the one hand, and a constructive, critical, self-reflective view of art on the other. The latter is the more difficult path; and it is this path, which requires both work and active thought on the part of the beholder, that Kosuth invited his viewers to follow. That so many people should have accepted the invitation is a tribute to his skills, and testimony to the urgency of the issues. It was as if people realized that what concerned them most deeply and touched them most profoundly could not be edited out by the dictates of government and by the officers of institutionalized morality.

Kosuth's art, like that of his fellow conceptual artists, does not lie simply in the production of a painting or a sculpture. For him, art is prior to its material; it is constituted by the very process of its being questioned, and is therefore wholly dependent on context. Being an artist means questioning the nature of *art*, not of painting or sculpture. The work of art, as he puts it, "is essentially a play within the meaning system of art." That play within the system is fundamentally predicated on the historical and social context of the individual viewer, and so the artist has necessarily to concern himself with philosophy, anthropology, psychology, and history. Indeed, for all his rejection of painting and sculpture as viable art forms now, and for all the fierceness of his critique of the institution of art history, there are few contemporary artists whose commitment to history runs as deep as Kosuth's. For him the power of the work we see in museums is derived from the concrete experience of the historical moment, both present and past. In short, "no matter what actual form the activity of art takes, its history gives it a concrete presence."

Kosuth's positions have been worked out over a long period in a series of notable essays, many of which have a direct bearing on the way in which the Brooklyn installation was conceived and presented. The phases of his work have often been presented as being comparatively disjunct, but in fact they follow logically one from the other. If the lodestar of the early phase was the philosophy of Wittgenstein, that of the second phase was radical anthropology, and that of the third the psychology of Freud. Yet Kosuth's engagement with each of these disciplines is unimaginable without the others. Throughout, the commitment to the role of art within the political and moral life has remained unwavering. For these reasons it is impossible to grasp either the impact of the Brooklyn installation or its place within his work without a brief consideration of the evolution of his thought.

In a famous essay of 1969 entitled "Art after Philosophy," Kosuth worked out the consequences of the view that works of art are akin to analytic propositions in language. The crucial proposal was that the work of art, like an analytic proposition (and unlike a synthetic proposition), contains no reference to any matter of fact beyond itself. Its validity is not dependent on any empirical, much less any aesthetic presupposition about the nature of things. Art precedes its material. It is tautological, like an analytic proposition, in that it contains its definition within itself. The artist's nomination of the work as "art" is what makes it art. In these respects, art is essentially linguistic in character (Kosuth would later modify this position by claiming, in line with the later Wittgenstein, that a defining characteristic of art is that it can show that which words can not say). Such a position has serious implications not only for the future of art, but also for its past. The difficulty with modernist painting and sculpture is that it exists solely in the realm of aesthetics and is essentially decorative. Since it refers to that which is beyond art (aesthetics), it does not add to our understanding of the nature of art. Worse still, since modernism became institutionalized and fetishized rather swiftly (as one might have predicted), it simply shored up the tradition, the conventional art histories, and—above all—the market.

Much of this may seem to be at a considerable remove from the Brooklyn installation, but it is less so than one might think. For Kosuth, the notion that we can only understand art as the *context* of art was as fundamental to his work in 1990 as it was in 1969. Of course, as Kosuth noted then, any object is eligible for aesthetic consideration once it is presented in, say, a museum; but because what makes art is its definition, what gives it its meaning—just like language—is its use.

Kosuth links his political agenda with his concern for the nature and concept of art thus: we cannot ignore the link between politics and the concept of art precisely because the presentation of the work in the museum or gallery is an ideological position, by the very fact of its institutionalization. I would add that the catch lies in the play between our own responses to the objects as objects, referring to the world of facts beyond them, and our responses to the objects understood (by virtue of denomination or installation) as works of art. We must also allow the discomfort of the never-ending cancellation of one response by the other, and acknowledge that it is from such discomfort or irritation that we achieve a form of understanding.

In the course of the next few years, Kosuth developed his thinking on the fundamental problem of context under the influence of Marxism and radical anthropology. The 1975 essay entitled "The Artist as Anthropologist" is, of all his earlier writings, perhaps the most directly relevant to the Brooklyn installation. Throughout it he constantly returns to his belief that the meaning of the work is constituted by the individual beholder. The first implication of this position is that we ought to renounce the old Cartesian distinction between experience and reality. The only reality is experienced reality: we cannot stop the emotions from interfering with the judgments that supposedly form the basis of scientific knowledge, and we must acknowledge the repression of sensuality under the domination of rationality. Objectivity can only be conceived of as alienation: the pressures of institutionalization to suppress what is most meaningful to us should be resisted. Hence the need to examine as critically as possible the ways in which fashion and the market determine our taste. Consumption and the fetishization of art as commodity reduce the autonomy of our judgment. It is imperative to remain as attentive as possible to "the sway of society over the inner life of the person," as William Leiss, one of Kosuth's great anthropologist heroes, puts it.

And so we begin to understand Kosuth's need to single out works that are not, as he later phrased it, part of the great *Autobahn* of masterpieces. "Lesser" or less famous works offer a better chance for us to form independent judgments, since the potential of such works is less likely to have been corrupted by their having been institutionalized, commodified, and turned into fetishes. For in his effort—his desire—to avoid reality, the fetishist focuses his attention on what is secondary. This, then, was another advantage of making a selection of works from the collections of The Brooklyn Museum. One could hardly fall into the trap of thinking, as a distinguished modern art historian once did, that "the superior craftsman, and only the superior one, is so organized that he can register within his medium an individual awareness of a period predicament." The fact is that even the undistinguished craftsman is likely to be able to register within his medium the period predicament, whether seen "individually" or as reflection of some common consciousness. If ever one needed evidence of the authority of "lesser" works of art as historical documents, it was to be found in Kosuth's installation.

But the issue went far beyond history and documentation; it forced a reevaluation of ourselves and our relation to present culture. In "The Artist as Anthropologist," Kosuth sought to show why one had not only to acquire fluency in a culture, but also to diminish the spurious distance, imposed by a false scientism, between oneself and that culture. Radical anthropology renounced the notion of the objective investigator; in the same way as one examined other cultures, one had to examine one's position within one's own culture. There are abundant lessons to be learned from other cultures, to be sure, but most important is to perceive the subjectivity of our own ideology, and the failure of objectivity. The duality between subject and object which permeates the "objectivity" of so much Western thought is only an impediment to understanding the inquiring

43

self itself and, therefore, to understanding the object of its investigation. And, as The Brooklyn Museum show demonstrates, since art only exists in context and as context, it becomes a critical implement not only in the activity of self-reflection, but also—and thereby—in the liberation from the constraints of fashion, taste, and the dictates of dominant social structures.

To say this may be to invest too much faith in the possibilities of art; but the moral dimension of Kosuth's work proposes that, with religion no longer viable, and with science doomed to its positivisms, we must turn to art for the understanding of ethics, value, and those issues of meaning that go beyond the laws of physics and the decrees of God.

Kosuth's concern with the role of the viewer soon led, naturally enough, to an intense engagement with the work of Sigmund Freud. Through Freud, Kosuth seems to have grown increasingly aware of the ways in which an individual beholder's contexts change, and of how meanings are lost, canceled, reclaimed, and revised in the light of personal experience. The opening quotation in his notes on the work entitled *Cathexis* came from Freud's 1915 paper on the Unconscious: "Thought proceeds in systems so far remote from the original perceptual residues that they have no longer retained anything of the qualities of those residues, and, in order to become conscious, need to be reinforced by new qualities."

This provides an important clue to the way in which Kosuth conceived of the Brooklyn provocation. His aim was to make the beholder as self-conscious as possible about the relation between conditions of context and the production of meaning. And he did so by making one as aware as possible of the *process* whereby meaning is constructed. The viewer begins to see the work of art in the way the artist does, "as a struggle to make and cancel meaning and re-form it." Understanding the work of art becomes an event that both locates and includes the viewer through the innumerable evocations, cancellations, and superimpositions called forth by the juxtaposition of objects and texts—in this case, in the domain of the "unmentionable."

One further element in Kosuth's conception of art and artwork bears directly on the Brooklyn installation—his view of the problem of the artwork's aura. He derived it, of course, from that maverick early associate of the Frankfurt school, Walter Benjamin.

For Benjamin, the aura of a work of art—and he was thinking particularly of painting—was tied to notions of authenticity and uniqueness. In an age of religion (or magic), aura was provided by ritual context (ritual space, the ritualization of tradition, or some combination of both); but in what he terms the age of mechanical reproduction, "the criterion of authenticity ceases to be applicable to artistic production [and] the total function of art is reversed. Instead of being based on ritual, it begins to be based on another practice—politics." Aura had become a nostalgic bourgeois category. The context that endowed the work with aura had now become the institutions of capitalist society, such as the museum and, mutatis mutandis, the market. Kosuth recognized the factitious aura of painting and the extent to which it was a product of hegemonic institutions—and so he gave it up. For him, the whole of art became the questioning of art. A truly political art, he realized, would not content itself with the message alone; it would —it had to—engage the viewer in a questioning of the nature and process of art itself. Only in this way could we understand the nature of the institutions and the pressures they exert, and thereby subject them to the necessary critique. For Kosuth, then, an art such as Hans Haacke's—in which the message lies primarily in the content—simply reinforces the positions already held by his viewers. It is too unambiguous. It cannot change any-

45

one because it fails to question its status as art and, therefore, its institutional presumptions and presuppositions.

This is the essential background to "The Play of the Unmentionable." This is how a major conceptual artist came to select a series of historical works of art from a major museum in order to make a political intervention that, although less obviously theoretical than much of his previous work, was wholly in keeping with the concerns of his practice.

"The Play of the Unmentionable" was an extraordinary success: over ninety-one thousand visitors came to visit the installation in the space of a little over three months. At any given time, the Grand Lobby of the museum—a large space of over eight thousand square feet—was unusually crowded. In recent years the Museum has done everything to ensure that this would not simply be empty space, in the way that grand museum lobbies often are; but now it took on an aspect that was both animated and intense. One had the distinct impression that the visitors to the installation were not simply making their way across the space to the main galleries of the museum, or to the exhibition of the works of Albert Pinkham Ryder that ran, also successfully, for the duration of the installation. They were concentrating, engaged in the issues so clearly presented by the images and mosaics of texts written with calculated elegance across the walls—beside, over, and under the objects. Kosuth's habitual skill in the presentation of texts made the installation seem at the same time eminently accessible and deeply provocative.

While several of Kosuth's preceding installations adopted similar strategies, none had enjoyed the same popular success. In comparison with the Brooklyn installation, the Wittgenstein exhibit in Vienna and Brussels would have seemed rather esoteric, both for its texts and for the difficult works it showed. Not that Kosuth would apologize for such difficulty: he has never claimed that art is, or should be, easy. But in the Brooklyn installation the stakes were plain, and they were revealed in the context of works that were clearly a part of our own history.

All this proved to be a seductive strategy. In most cases it required no great initial leap to understanding. The works were generally ones that formed part of the traditions and conventions we know. But Kosuth's juxtapositions and the spatial and intellectual intervention of the texts set an unexpected kind of mental effort in motion. One found oneself meditating on the relations between objects, between objects and texts, and between objects, texts, and oneself. Constantly one sought to construct the work, as work of art, below the fragments of other discourses. By using texts, "the mystified experience of aesthetic contemplation was ruptured." Because texts, as Kosuth insists, are human marks, and since language is daily and banal "the individualizing profundity of contemplation was denied." As he affirmed with regard to his earlier work, *Cathexis*, "the viewer, as a reader, could experience the language of the construction of what is seen. That cancellation of habituated experiences which makes the language visible also forces the viewers/readers to realize their own subjective role in the meaning-making process."

As a result, one could hardly have failed to see that there are no intrinsic meanings in an object or an image, but that meaning always exists in relation to the viewer, as well as "to society, and in relation to what preceded it, to what it shares, and to what follows." Soon one could see that meanings were being produced that went beyond the overt content of the works. We, as viewers, were made aware of *our* role in the production of meaning, and the old mystifying, transcendental status of art was broken. We could grasp the full extent of art's embeddedness in history and culture, and in

47

this manner be led to engage the issues of censorship, control, and the limits of art. For they, too, could now clearly be seen as subject to determination by context, period, and convention. They were as inabsolute as the transcendence of art. The unmentionable was revealed through the play of the unmentionable and through the processes by which meanings are constructed and made apparent. Every beholder was made conscious of the processes whereby history and context interact with the individual. And art could show what words alone could not say.

Nor could any visitor to the Brooklyn installation have had any doubt that one was dealing with a new work, one by Kosuth. This was not just another exhibition of individual works of art, curated by an art historian or museum curator in such a way as to leave our sense of the autonomy of art objects and their historical distance unimpinged (let alone unthreatened). The exhibition was clearly dialectical. Individual works were actualized, as it were: because the production of meaning lay so clearly with the viewer, the artworks were charged with meanings and implications they had never had before. Or, to put it more precisely, the objects were charged with meanings that had lain dormant in them, waiting, one might say, to be awakened under the conditions of both Kosuth's work and the historical moment in which it was set.

The challenge became obvious as soon as one entered the museum. For one thing, there were the texts. Printed in white lettering on gray walls, in various typesizes, they arrested one's attention, both for their form and their content. The large, banner-style slogans captured the eye, drawing it down to the longer sentences, and then to the paragraphs, inscribed in the smallest print around discrete clusters of objects and images. The texts insisted that we read them. There was no need to search, as we sometimes anxiously do, for the innocuous and "objective" labels that we generally need as historical crutches with which to look more safely (or less igno-rantly) upon works that we do not know or have not seen before, or that come from another period. These "labels" were comments, provocations, insults, puzzles, contradictions, and stimulations. One was impelled into a personal interaction with each text, and with each image or object on which the text commented—if one had not already been forced into some interaction by the strength or unusualness of the object itself.

The provocation—like the challenge to see uniquely—also began immedi-ately, with the inscription of the title of the installation on the entrance wall of the Grand Lobby. "The Brooklyn Museum Collection: The Play of the Unmentionable." The series of oxymorons, of contradictions, had started off: museum/*play*/unmentionable: these are not the usual or the conventional collocations. Beneath this title came a frank acknowledge-ment of the support of the National Endowment for the Arts. The mighty second museum of New York! The greatest grant-giving body in the field of the arts! What place could there be for the unmentionable within these institutions—one erected by virtuous citizenry as the very embodiment of the relations between knowledge, art, and authority, and the other nothing less than an arm of government? Off to the left one caught a glimpse of a picture of a naked man and a variety of sculptures of nude young men (pp. 88–93). Revealing himself, as it were, from behind, the man in the picture seemed casually to be attending to some need (he turned out to be lighting a cigarette) of a seated clothed figure (p. 91). Off to the right one could make out three large oil paintings of more or less unclothed children (pp. 111–113).

The Cincinnati trial, which began the day before the opening of "The Play of the Unmentionable" at The Brooklyn Museum, revolved around a

49

well-known homosexual artist's photographs of men in sadomasochistic poses, and of children with their genitals exposed. The coincidence of dates was by chance and not by design, of course; but for months—as everyone knew—the NEA had been equivocating, vacillating, and finally submitting in the face of pressure not to fund, directly or indirectly, the production or exhibition of artworks representing the supposedly unmentionable. But who decides? This must have been at least one of the many questions that now entered into play.

To have opened with the *most* famous of the passages by that great philosopher of liberty, Jean-Jacques Rousseau ("man is born free but is everywhere in chains"), would have been too obvious; but it was powerfully alluded to by the first three images in the installation: Barbara Kruger's *We are notifying you of a change of address*, where heavy chains both imprison and bar access to an apparently bare female figure (p. 72); Lucas Cranach the Elder's *Lucretia* with a large chain around her neck, as she stabs herself in shame at her rape (p. 73); and finally Hiram Powers's *Greek Slave*, with the heavy chain that both enslaves her and seems to preserve her chastity (p. 73). These are such contradictory choices that they force us to work to resolve them. Alongside the images came the opening quotation, not the obvious one by the philosopher of Geneva, but another, even more germane:

> The savage lives within himself, while social man lives constantly outside himself and knows only how to live in the opinion of others, so that he seems to receive the consciousness of his own existence merely from the judgement of others concerning him.

Reminders of *their* autonomy and *our* slavishness would henceforth punctuate the installation. We had embarked on the difficult search for the integrity within ourselves, by being made to reflect on the process of artistic activity and on the implications of our own definition of art. The constant issue would be our independence of judgment: who, Kosuth seemed insistently to be asking, decided what was or was not art, and what follows from that decision? Freedom and tolerance, or control and censorship?

At the same time, though, there was another issue, that of the nature of artistic activity and its legitimate domain. In calling attention to the Koranic parallels between the creative powers of the artist and those of God himself, the text that immediately followed the opening cluster of images presented all too clearly the threat of artistic autonomy to institutional power, and the need to control the freedom that comes from creation.

> On the Day of Judgement the punishment of hell will be meted out to the painter, and he will be called upon to breathe life into the forms that he has fashioned; but he cannot breathe life into anything. In fashioning the form of a being that has life, the painter is usurping the creative function of the Creator and thus is attempting to assimilate himself to God...

To make what one likes, and to be free to do so, is to aspire to a power that is not of the human realm, because it is the power to make images vital. This is the threat that the lawmakers cannot tolerate, because it is the guarantor of the potential of our resistance to control.

But what are the further implications of this freedom—to make what one likes and to be free to do so—and of the varieties of constraints that are placed upon it? While the Islamic proscriptions may be concerned with the dangers of aspiring to creative powers that only God is supposed to have, what is it in the West that constrains freedom? In "The Artists as Anthropologist," Kosuth cites William Leiss on the ways in which the transformation of all of nature (including consciousness itself) into the material of production comes to be "compulsive, blindly repetitive and finally self-destructive." For Leiss, "the final stage is reached when the only rationale for production that can be offered is that many persons can be induced to believe that what they really want and need are the newest offering of commodities in the marketplace." This is the most insidious constraint on artistic freedom. Whether or not we now take such a bleak view of the effects of the marketplace, it is not hard to grasp the lesson here, and it is phrased in such a way as to serve as a perfect motto for "The Play of the Unmentionable":

> At this stage domination over nature and men, directed by the ruling social class, becomes internalized in the psychic process of individuals; and it is self-destructive because the compulsive character of consumption and behavior destroys personal autonomy and negates the long and difficult effort to win liberation from that experience of external compulsion.

This is a complex and important point; but one can perhaps speak still more bluntly and plainly, just as Kosuth himself does. The Brooklyn installation, as we have seen, was conceived as a direct response to recent assaults on freedom of expression and artistic liberty. The situation was all too clear. The NEA had refused to give grants to works that it, in its wisdom, had decided were immoral or pornographic; the Corcoran Galley in Washington had, at the last minute, canceled a show of photographs by Robert Mapplethorpe; and the Cincinnati trial was about to open. The issue of what an artist could or could not do—should or should not be allowed to do—was on the minds of many more people than usual. Under these circumstances, photographs such as those by Larry Clark could only have been taken as some kind of deliberate provocation (pp. 95, 107–10, 141). Beside them, photographs by Mapplethorpe such as the one on display from The Brooklyn Museum collection must have seemed altogether innocuous and tame, slick and decorative (p. 92). One has no difficulty in finding in them just those formal qualities that seem to be so lacking in Clark (though, as always, there is no shortage of people willing to offer a formal analysis of *his* works too).

The depiction of sex in Larry Clark's photographs seems plain and explicit enough. Even the more sophisticated viewers, upon seeing them for the first time, are likely to ask themselves (or at least, to entertain the thought): Can these works really be *art*? And if they are, what then are the conditions of art? These are exactly the questions that Kosuth wants us to raise. The whole of his own art is about this. It is not just that he brings out of storage a painting of an apparently homosexual exchange, showing a wholly nude male figure (the model for *Prometheus*!) with an attractive rump (p. 91), or coy pictures of seminude children (pp. 111–113), in order to bring the very issues that were most debated in 1990 to mind. It is that his use of context and contextualization is so effective.

For example, in confronting us with Larry Clark's picture of a boy handling his penis (p. 95), and setting it in the visual context of the Roman statues of Dionysus and Apollo (pp. 90, 93), he makes us face the possibility that we may be more aware than we like to admit about the absence of the male member (whether lost by chance or by deliberate mutilation) in the antique works. Or that we may either be more sensitive to, or more inclined to suppress, the sexual aspects of the Egyptian bronze (p. 94) of a Pharaoh worshiping the Otter (which he does, we may not immediately notice, with a phallus attached to his forehead and by masturbating as he worships).

We have no difficulty in classifying these Egyptian, Greek, and Roman works as art, and we tolerate their sexual dimension by suppressing our interest in it; but with Larry Clark....? In the case of the ancient statues it all seems much clearer. Either we do not notice the sexual dimension because the objects are in a museum, and because art permits us to repress that which would trouble us in an object we are more reluctant to admit as art— or we simply *pretend* not to notice. From the Rodin bronzes (pp. 100–101) to the Japanese woodblock albums (pp. 104–106), these were the issues that "The Play of the Unmentionable" brought constantly, insistently, and trenchantly to the fore.

In a direct allusion to one of the Mapplethorpe photographs singled out by the Cincinnati prosecution, Kosuth showed a Mughal painting *Intoxicated Ascetics* (p. 103), the central scene of which is a man urinating directly into the mouth of another. Kosuth did not hesitate to have an enlargement made of this scene, as if in defiance of all "scientific" art-historical commentary, which has never commented directly on it (even though the page itself is well-enough known). It is reported to be an illustration of the fastest way of allowing opium to enter the bloodstream; but once we have *this* information, there is yet another problem, yet another aspect of the play of the unmentionable. Are we somehow supposed to feel that historical knowledge—essentially *social* knowledge—somehow detracts from the transcendental status of art? Or does it have nothing to do with art at all?

The other photographs by Larry Clark present similar difficulties. Kosuth showed these images of adolescent sex in the company of three paintings of disrobed children and a pair of textual reminders by myself— the first about the barrier against regarding realism as art ("Art is beautiful and high. The photograph is realistic; it is vulgar; it elicits natural and realistic responses. In art, nudity is beautiful and ideal; in the photograph (unless it has acquired the status of art), it is ugly and (therefore?) provocative"), and the second about the contextuality of pornography ("Arousal by image [whether pornographic or not] only occurs in context: in the

54

context of the individual beholder's conditioning, and, as it were, of his preparation for seeing the arousing, erotic, or pornographic image. It is dependent on the prior availability of images and prevailing boundaries of shame," etc.). But beside the oil paintings he also inscribed in large letters a passage from the biography of William Sergeant Kendall, the painter of the picture evasively called *A Statuette* (p. 113). "Americans," wrote Kendall's biographer, "have never felt entirely comfortable with paintings of the nude. Perhaps Kendall's nudes were so well liked because they showed children and were therefore removed from a sexual context." While the first part of this passage may be a fair acknowledgment of a certain state of affairs, the evasiveness of the second only became fully apparent in the context of the Larry Clarks.

But with evasion comes great illumination. It is as hard to believe in the absence of sexual content in Kendall's (seminude) painting of a child as it is to deny that our discomfort with Larry Clark's photographs, however enlightened we may be, springs precisely from the unadorned adolescent sexuality they portray, as well as from our persistent reluctance to integrate sex and art. Kosuth's installation spoke for itself—one had only to survey the history of art to see that they need not be seen as contradictory in terms. At the same time, though, it raised the question: What is the force of institutionalization that impels the separation of these categories? This was the motor that drove Kosuth's selection of works from the Brooklyn collection, a selection sanctioned by the authority of the very institution that had collected them. This, in short, was the paradox that provoked.

We may think a representation pornographic, or acknowledge that others are likely to think it pornographic. We know that this judgment, this assignment of category, is wholly dependent on context, convention, and

55

education. But how is this judgment affected by the knowledge that the work is a work of art, or even by the *suspicion* that it may be? *Who*, after all, determines? And how is autonomy of judgment affected by the determination of the work as art? It may be that in making his spectators reflect more on the question of the concept of art than on the narrowness of censorship, Kosuth overstated the problem—*his* favored problem. But one must acknowledge the prescience of his demonstration that the very act of social control manifested as censorship is that it is nothing more than an extension of power into the domain of autonomy embodied in the idea of art. And indeed, his prescience was clearly vindicated by the proceedings and the outcome of the trial in Cincinnati.

From the very start of the trial, it was clear that the central issue would be the artistic status of the seven photographs. The fundamental question was: Could such (pornographic) images possibly be regarded as art? The lead prosecutor would show and describe every photograph and ask each member of the jury: "Is this art?" Of course, the prosecution's hope was that the jury would see that the photos could not possibly be art (since art is pure, transcendent, culturally and spiritually enhancing, and so on). As in the early days of photography, if the image was too realistic it could not be art. But to the prosecution the matter must have seemed clear, even if tautologous: if it is art, it is art, but if it is pornography, it is not art. The prosecution cannot long have considered the possibility that someone might demonstrate the contrary. And yet someone, many people, did. The jury was swayed by those authorities (museum officials and critics) who convinced them that the images were art—and therefore not pornographic. Now the legal position was clear, and was set forth with surprising lucidity by a judge whom everyone had taken to be hostile to the museum's case. The threefold test of obscenity was "that the average person applying contemporary community standards would find that the picture, taken as a whole, appeals to a prurient interest in sex, that the picture depicts or describes sexual conduct in a patently offensive way, and that the picture, taken as a whole, lacks serious literary, artistic, political, or scientific value."

Yet it is impossible not to feel a little uneasy at the facility of the outcome. If the members of the jury genuinely believed, at the outset, that the images were pornographic (say, sexually stimulating in a way that presented some kind of danger to public morality), how could they suddenly have changed their minds just because the images were nominated as art? How does the category of art come to have such power—if indeed it has this power—to alter perceptions? And on whose say-so are such images thus nominated? Do they become art only when they enter a museum? The temptation is to suggest that it was a moral failing of the jury not to retain their independence of judgment, stay with their sense of the pornographic, and refuse to be swayed by the fact that the director of the J. Paul Getty Museum, the director of the University Art Museum at Berkeley, and the former director of the Institute of Contemporary Art of the University of Pennsylvania (and current director of the American Craft Museum) all declared that these images were art. Could not at least one member of the jury have responded, as the prosecutor presumably did, by saying (or at least thinking): "Whatever you claim, I think these images are pornographic"? And could he or she in that case not have resisted adding "and therefore certainly not art"?

Here lies one crux of the matter. But there is another, just as crucial, in what we now may take to have been an unexpected triumph for the position demonstrated by Kosuth's work. That is, it can only have been a sense of the contextuality of pornography that made the jury refuse the obvious position: Once pornography always pornography. "The picture [of the girl with her skirt up] is a perfect illustration of the phrase 'Evil is in the eye of the beholder,' " concluded the art critic of the *Cincinnati Enquirer.* "Who determines what is a work of art?" asked the prosecutor. "It's the culture at large—museums, critics, galleries. No one person makes the determination. It's more than personal, more than local," replied an expert witness. To refuse the position "once pornography always pornography," as we shall see, is neither to repudiate the power of images nor to deny their capacity to arouse. Nor is it, as some skeptics might claim, simply an indication of upward cultural mobility ("now we too can recognize what makes these images art").

One further aspect of both the proceedings and the jury's decision merits reflection. The jury seems to have been chiefly convinced by those critics who offered a formalist defense of the photographs (their strategy was to prove that the photos qualified as art on formal grounds, as if this were the sole possible basis for proof). Could such a jury, consisting of ordinary members of the Cincinnati community, really have been persuaded, almost overnight, by arguments such as those regarding the figure study of the photographer with a bullwhip in his anus? "The human figure is centered. The horizon line is two-thirds of the way up, almost the classical two-thirds to one-third proportion. The way the light is cast so there is light all around the figure [is] very symmetrical, which is very characteristic of his flowers...." Surely, one might have thought that this was too fancy a diversion from the reality of the image? Apparently not. The trump card was provided by the most adept of the formal analysts who, when asked, "So when you look at a picture, you look at it differently?" replied emphatically, "No! Training in art is just training in life, really."

One could hardly have wished for a more spectacular vindication of the strategy of "The Play of the Unmentionable." If anyone thought that

Kosuth had overestimated the importance of the question of art, the result of the Cincinnati trial (and the relaxation of restrictions by the NEA that followed in its wake) proved that he had not. It was precisely *their own* reflection on "the historical relationship between the artist and the concept of art in this society" that made members of the jury realize the impossibility and futility of censorship.

The jury was swayed by an exposition of the formal aspects of the works at issue. Apparently, either one meaning of the work was set aside or, as a result of their questioning of the nature of art, form became meaning (or, at least, integral to it). One might not have predicted that a jury of people not normally involved with the making or business of art would be moved by formal arguments—and yet they were. This can only mean that both the art establishment and the anti-art establishment misjudge the involvement of most museumgoers with issues of art. But was the day saved only because the works were proved to be art? Once again the question returns: Who decides? We know well enough that at Cincinnati it was the directors of the museums. We could take this as just one further sign of the institutionalization of the radical, which has become so complex an aspect of the cultural politics of our times. But it also seems to mean that Mapplethorpe is now safely institutionalized. Could this be why Kosuth insisted on the inclusion of the photographs by Larry Clark? Beside him, as I have noted, Mapplethorpe's works look a little too smooth, stylish, and marketable.

But here lies a considerable irony. For all his assaults on the connection between style and the market, Kosuth's own work betrays an extreme degree of what might roughly be called high formalization. It is cool and elegant, and its junctures of words, light, and visuality are almost seamlessly consistent. Initially, in his work Kosuth sought a certain neutrality of

59

presentation. Lettering was intended to be undistinctive, rather than overtly "artistic." But, whether or not he intended it, even this neutrality gained its own historical momentum and status with the passage of time. The result, ironically enough, has been a distinctive Kosuthian style. We see it in the Brooklyn installation as much as in his other works. And it has, inevitably, become eminently marketable. The artist has been caught on the very hook that he so effectively baited.

At least two more paradoxes, or problems, arise from Kosuth's thinking. To overlook them would be an abnegation of the very candor his art demands. After the paradox of institutionalization come those of contextuality and aura. They are less obviously paradoxical, but equally relevant to the effectiveness of the installation. They are paradoxical for two reasons: the strength of the installation could be seen to depend, at least to some extent, on a community of response that somehow infringes the rule of contextuality (as is now most obvious in the case of images that are seen to carry a sexual charge); and the power of its images appeared to depend on a quality that might once have been described as aura, had it not been for the critique that Benjamin based on the commodification and institutionalization of art.

In my book *The Power of Images* I emphasized the poverty of a view of the history of art that does not take the constitutive role of the viewer into full consideration, whether for the meaning or the power of images. I argued that it is impossible to understand either the present or the past of images unless one takes the active role of the viewer into account. And I suggested that one means of gaining access to the dialectic of interaction is by plotting and investigating the symptoms of responses, however troubling and difficult, to art and to images. Such an investigation seems feasible only if it is based not simply on the internal history of images, but

60

also on the application of the lessons of philosophy, anthropology, and psychology.

My trajectory, therefore, is not dissimilar to Kosuth's; we have a kindred sense of the constructive and the limiting roles of context. It is instructive that, as if in alarm at my delineation of responses which intellectuals in general, and art historians in particular, either deny or seek to banish from their territories, choruses of art-historical fear arose. These choruses were reinforced by two anxieties. First, predictably enough, there was the fear that I was somehow reducing the status of art by suggesting that we recall our responses to everyday imagery when we investigate our responses to what we regard as art; and, secondly, there was the anxiety that I was attributing to images some mysterious power, and thereby failing to acknowledge individual needs and the projection of individual desires. I mention these reactions because they offer some insight into the premises of Kosuth's practice, specifically that of "The Play of the Unmentionable."

As we have seen, Kosuth repeatedly insists on the operative role of the viewer, his or her *constitutive* role. There are no intrinsic meanings—no intrinsic *power*, I would add—in objects and images. It is the viewer who must struggle for the meaning of art, in the face of the dictates of market and institutions. Some critics of *The Power of Images* were apparently so afraid of the responses to art that might thus arise that they compounded their fears by suggesting that I attributed the power of images to images themselves, autonomously and therefore somehow magically—the very position I had repeatedly sought to undermine. Such is the power invested in images, it would seem, that even my repeated acknowledgement of the necessity of context renewed the old fears that they might have an inherent power of their own.

The days of belief in the passive spectator are now happily over; and only the most intransigent believers in the absolute transcendence of great works of art or the staunchest proponents of the market's determining role lament their passing. But that forlorn position has recently come to be replaced by a positivism, that, though it has been nurtured by the worthiest of motives, has become the domain of the fearful and the timid: the positivism of small context, of anecdote, of the narrow forms of what has fashionably come to be called "microhistory."

Granted that the viewer constructs the meaning of the work; but how is the viewer himself or herself constructed? This is the question that has led many astray. The attentive and up-to-date reader may already have raised at least one eyebrow at the ways in which both Kosuth and I sometimes refer to "people," or "the viewer," or make use of the generalized first-person plural. To do so is neither to hypostatize "the viewer" nor to sacrifice individuality for the sake of some kind of corporate response. It is not to minimize difference, nor to say that everyone responds in the same way to a given work or set of circumstances. Rather, it *is* to point up those common bases of response, emotion, and cognition upon which context acts and whose very commonality makes them amenable to analysis. We have no good words for them. They relate to hunger, sexuality, grief, gladness, terror. They are those awkward facts of feeling, instinct, and desire that have their roots in our humanity. Of course, these categories are themselves inflected by context, and subject to social and gender construction—always. Prior to such inflection we must reckon with whatever it is that enables arousal and emotion. To say this is to do no more than declare the work that has still to be done: theoretical on the one hand, technical on the other. While different images may arouse the sexual feelings of different people at different times under different circumstances, it would be futile not to acknowledge the cognitive process, prior to context, that enables arousal by representation; and because this is a process that is prior to context, it cannot be named (except, perhaps, in neurophysiological terms). It is a theoretical construct with physiological reality.

One cannot understand the desire to censor without understanding desire *tout court*—specifically the desire for what is represented. However much context shapes content, and however much one acknowledges that standards of morality, when applied to art, are wholly determined by socio-historical context and the varieties of conditioning, the link between vision and desire nevertheless remains to be excavated and theorized.

For the sake of argument, let us say one attributes the greater popular success of the Brooklyn installation (in comparison with the 1989 Wittgenstein installation, "The Play of the Unsayable") to the fact that people are more interested in the unmentionable than the unsayable. But to maintain such a position these days causes scandal, and it is not hard to imagine Kosuth himself, the artist as anthropologist, objecting on the grounds that there is no such thing as "people" in general, only different people and different contexts. But it is clear enough that the installation would have failed had not every spectator been able to recognize the sexual charge of the Larry Clarks, or the savagery of Cindy Sherman (p. 134) and the slicing off of the breasts of the Spanish Saint Agatha (p. 137); or the pricking of the needles in Clark's *First Time Shooting Up* (p. 141), Norman Rockwell's 1944 *The Tattoo Artist* (p. 141), and the Nkisi power figure (p. 140); or the deprivation of vitality betokened by the willful removal of the eyes of a figure in a picture such as the fifteenth-century *Martyrdom of Saints Cosmas and Damian with their Three Brothers* (p. 129), where the eyes were presumably scratched at the time of the iconoclastic disturbances of the next century in an attempt to deprive the executioners of their malevolent life or vitality.

63

Of course, there are plenty of other aspects of the "Play of the Unmentionable" that would have been incomprehensible in other contexts; but the power of the installation resided precisely in the degree to which it forced its spectators to reflect on the ways in which they judged the inflection of response by context. Of course, one might also claim that its effectiveness depended wholly on the common cultural identity of its spectators—but in Brooklyn, of all places? The argument would be a weak one. No more representative microcosm of the world could we know. The installation forced one to reflect on context; but it depended for its effectiveness on a cognitive grasp of the roots of emotion, appetite, and fear: fear of oneself as much as fear of the other.

In *The Power of Images* I was chiefly concerned with the power that arises in the case of all imagery, and not only in those images we call "art." Kosuth, however, in the Brooklyn installation took one important step further: he decided to use the power of images as a means of understanding the power of art. While the role of the viewer in making meaning is fundamental to both his and my own aims, Kosuth's breakthrough was to take the step from representation in general to art itself.

"The meaning of art is how we *describe* it. The *description of art*—which art itself manifests—consists of a dynamic cluster of uses, shifting from work to work, of elements taken from the very fabric of culture—no different from those which construct reality day to day." On the basis of this position, Kosuth can make the most satisfactory claim we yet have for considering the role of the viewer as a means of insight into making. Viewers make meaning in the way artists make meaning: in both cases meaning is predicated on the questioning of art. Once one acknowledges the definition of art as a questioning, as a test rather than an illustration, one may

64

begin to see it in terms of its liberating possibilities. It is a (*the*) fundamentally unalienating activity precisely because it allows us to participate in the making of meaning rather than having it foisted on us by some outside force such as superior taste, the market, some august institution, or anything else we might accept unquestioningly. Finally, we are able to interrogate our own complicity.

To remember the lessons of the everyday and the ethnographic is to begin to understand the power of what we call "art." We fail to grasp the force of images in our culture because they have become anodyne from familiarity, and because of our constant inclination to repress. Who in a civilized society finds it easy to admit to the savage within ourselves, to responses that seem primitive, raw, and basic—the kind we think characteristic of other, more "primitive" cultures? As long as we think of art as no more than expensive decoration, no more than the unthinking "regurgitation of traditional forms ignorant of tradition," we will continue to think of form as pure and autonomous content; and the motivation to censor—as well as art's capacity to offend us (or them)—will continue to elude our grasp. If we fail to recognize the full extent to which art can go beyond the pleasing and the decorative, we fail to see the essential disturbances of art, and fetishize instead everything that is on its periphery: style, formalism, aesthetics, and those postmodernisms that are ignorant in their derivations.

And so the problem of aura remains. It remains a useful term, Benjamin's critique notwithstanding, for referring to the powers of images that we are inclined to repress, such as those that follow from the conflation of signifier and signified. Aura might also be applied usefully to those effects of images that were once clearer and easier to recognize in an age of ritual and religion. And it serves to underline the continuity between responses to religious images in the past and responses to other kinds of images now, including sexual ones. The corollary, of course, is that we fail to acknowledge the full effects of images because of the varieties of repression legitimized by art. But how to move from the power of images to the meaning of art?

There is, in Kosuth, a high faith in art: not in the art we unthinkingly accept, nor in the art of market or fashion, but rather in art that makes itself by questioning, describing, and defining itself. This, for him, is what replaces the old notion of aura. The viewer, not the ritual, makes the meaning of the work. Power comes from the active, dialectical engagement with the work and from the testing of its status as art. Aura was provided by religion in the past, by various cultural institutions now; but it has become an empty vessel. In an age of easy reproduction aura can only serve the interests of the market; and it does so, of course, by furthering the commodification of the object. Kosuth offers us the only compelling alternative. By replacing the fetishization of the object with reflection on the nature of art, and by showing the actual *work* involved in the process of reflection and questioning, he has reinstated the power of art. This power, in the end, is also a liberating one, because it encourages consciousness to become aware of itself and to recognize the forces that act upon it.

"The Play of the Unmentionable," therefore, is not only about censorship but also—above all—about the conditions of art. It brings to the fore censorship's direct dependence on how we and all other viewers think about the nature of art. Censorship is incapable of being programmed; it cannot be made into a set of immutable rules, precisely because it, like our notions of art, is wholly context dependent. Meaning is made by individual viewers in their context; it is not immanent in the objects of art. When we accept the meanings with which the institutions of our culture—whether market,

66

museum, or people "of superior taste"—endow the work, we relinquish some of our freedom. Kosuth shows how liberation can only come from the ceaseless questioning and requestioning of the nature of art. We ourselves make meaning in the way the best artists do, by never giving up that questioning. Only in this way can we challenge the sterile dominance of institutionally imposed taste. Art, in the end, is what art means to us. It opens to us one of the few roads to authenticity in a society that insists on imposing its taste at every turn and by every means—nowadays, above all, by the market. By means of the questioning on which Kosuth insists, by means of the interrogation of the nature of art, we at least make some progress in freeing our inner life from the sway of ideology. No wonder that Kosuth begins with Rousseau's critique of social man, who "lives constantly outside himself and only knows how to live in the opinion of others." Rousseau offers the savage as the model of authenticity; but what is really at stake here is authentic autonomy of judgment. Kosuth seeks to lay it bare not simply by insisting on the independent questioning of art, but by encouraging us to reflect on the ways in which other societies are capable of purer and more independent judgments—though, admittedly, also of similar sorts of social control—with the result that art retains some of the force it has lost in our own.

This loss of force is to be attributed not simply to the dominance of the institutions, but also to the irreversible historical fact that the society in which we live is no longer unified. This, for a start, is why works of art can no longer be pictures of the world. In a fragmented, nonunified society such as ours meanings necessarily differ from viewer to viewer. As we have repeatedly seen, it is the viewer in context who makes meaning—a meaning achieved by an attentiveness to the play within systems of meaning. "The Play of the Unmentionable" makes us see how meaning emerges from the interstices within the relations between relations, in such a way that we begin to discern still further relations not seen before. Meaning may be elicited by texts, but texts themselves are limited. Art says what texts cannot say. It offers to us the constructive elements for what can only be said indirectly, for the unsayable and even the unmentionable. Kosuth's achievement is to help us understand that art is more than its objects, that it resides in how we question the nature of art, and that understanding emerges from the play of relations. We can only begin the process of understanding if we open ourselves to that play and succeed in ridding ourselves of our socially determined preconceptions about the meanings of works.

Above all, however, Kosuth has succeeded in taking that most conservative of institutions, the museum, and turning it into a liberating place. As in the past, so too now, the museum has become a cathedral where we submissively pay homage to the dogmas of art, and where we either passively yield or actively embrace an orthodoxy imposed from on high. But for a brief period The Brooklyn Museum—with its complicity—became a place where meaning could be made as a result of critical thinking about the process and nature of art itself. For once, ironically enough, that meaning could be achieved free from the dictates of the institution itself, since the play of texts and objects allowed a play of the imagination unfettered by normal rules and constraints.

Once we censor, however, once we accept the full consequences of institutionalization and impose the rules and cancellations censorship demands, we exclude the possibility of art. That is both the threat of censorship and the challenge it poses, not merely to art but to the liberation art offers. This liberation is in turn the most essential, the most indispensable part of the nature of art. By refusing its dangers, censorship takes away art's possibility.

THE 'PLAY' DETAILED

The savage lives within himself, while social man lives constantly outside himself and only knows how to live in the opinion of others, so that he seems to receive the consciousness of his own existence merely from the judgement of others concerning him.

JEAN-JACQUES ROUSSEAU,
"A DISCOURSE ON THE ORIGIN AND FOUNDATION
OF INEQUALITY AMONG MEN"

BARBARA KRUGER
(AMERICAN, B. 1945)
Untitled
(We Are Notifying You of a Change of Address), 1986
UNIQUE PHOTOGAPH, 87.56
HELEN B. SAUNDERS FUND, CAROLINE A. L. PRATT FUND,
AND CHARLES S. SMITH MEMORIAL FUND

WORKSHOP OF LUCAS CRANACH THE ELDER
(GERMAN, 1472–1555)
Lucretia, C.1526–37
OIL ON PANEL, 21.142
BEQUEST OF A. AUGUSTUS HEALY

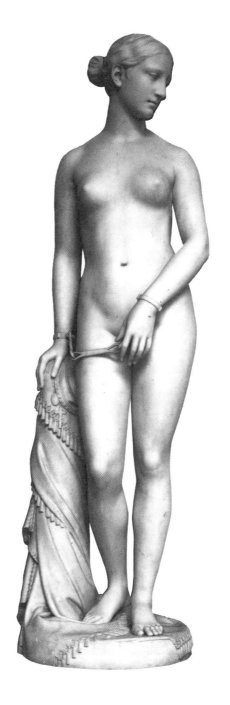

HIRAM POWERS
(AMERICAN, 1805–1873)
The Greek Slave, 1869
MARBLE, 55.14
GIFT OF CHARLES F. BOUND

73

M. Blair Coan, investigator for the Senatorial Vice Commission, popularly known as the "white slave commission," wasted no time in announcing that, in response to many complaints, he was instituting a personal and "thorough investigation" of the Exhibition. He later advised the press that, after having visited the Show and inspected the works, he found Futurist art immoral, that every girl in Chicago was gazing at examples of distorted art, and that one of the women in Matisse's *Le Lux* had four toes.

MILTON BROWN,
The Story of the Armory Show

"The body is the temple of God," said Charles Francis Browne to a ladies' group in Evanston, "and the cubists have profaned the temple." Arthur Burrage Farwell, president of the Chicago Law and Order League, warned: "It is a grave mistake to permit these pictures to hang either here or elsewhere. Why the saloons could not hang these pictures! There is a law prohibiting it. The idea that some people can gaze at this sort of thing without its hurting them is all bosh. This exhibition ought to be suppressed."

MILTON BROWN,
The Story of the Armory Show

PAUL GAUGUIN
(FRENCH, 1848–1903)
Tahitian Woman, C. 1891
PASTEL ON PAPER, 21.125
MUSEUM COLLECTION FUND

HENRI MATISSE
(FRENCH, 1869–1954)
Clearing at Malabai, C. 1916
OIL ON CANVAS, 67.24.16
BEQUEST OF LAURA L. BARNES

75

HENRI MATISSE
(FRENCH, 1869–1954)
Woman in an Armchair, c. 1916
OIL ON CANVAS, 67.24.15
BEQUEST OF LAURA L. BARNES

In a world of shifting values, the only thing the layman felt sure of, and unfortunately without foundation, was skill. But his very conception of skill made these objects incomprehensible. Harriet Monroe, still fighting off the inevitable conversion, wrote that Matisse seemed "fundamentally insincere" and that he talked "blague in a loud voice." The critic of the *Boston Transcript* found Matisse and the Cubists "playing a game of mystification." Mather gave his readers a choice: Cubism was either "a clever hoax or a negligible pedantry." Cox, not to be outdone, offered "sheer insanity or the triumphant charlatanry." In an attack on the Armory Show in the *Times* of March 22, he stated bluntly that up to the time of Matisse the artistic revolutionaries had at least been sincere, they had committed suicide or died in madhouses, but now they were making insanity pay.

MILTON BROWN,
The Story of the Armory Show

JACQUES VILLON
(FRENCH, 1875–1930)
Le Philosophe, 1930
OIL ON CANVAS, 34.1000
GIFT OF MRS. GERDA STEIN

77

GEORGES BRAQUES
(FRENCH, 1881–1963)
Fox, 1911
ETCHING AND DRYPOINT, 36.59
A. AUGUSTUS HEALY FUND

78

Shortly before the arrival of the Show, defenders of public morals had forced the removal from a dealer's window of a reproduction of Paul Chabas' *September Morn*, a typical French academic example of simpering nudity, and a Fraestad barnyard scene from the Art Institute. The situation was ripe for a crusade. "A clergyman," according to Walter Pach, "wrote to the newspapers that he had been obliged to turn back his flock of Sunday school children at the head of the stairs…[when] he saw from the door that the rooms were filled with the degeneracies of Paris; he demanded that the public be protected from them as he had protected his children." A high-school teacher announced that the Exhibition was "nasty, lewd, immoral, and indecent." When questioned, the superintendent of schools let it be known that he was considering declaring the Show off-limits for school children.

MILTON BROWN,
The Story of the Armory Show

79

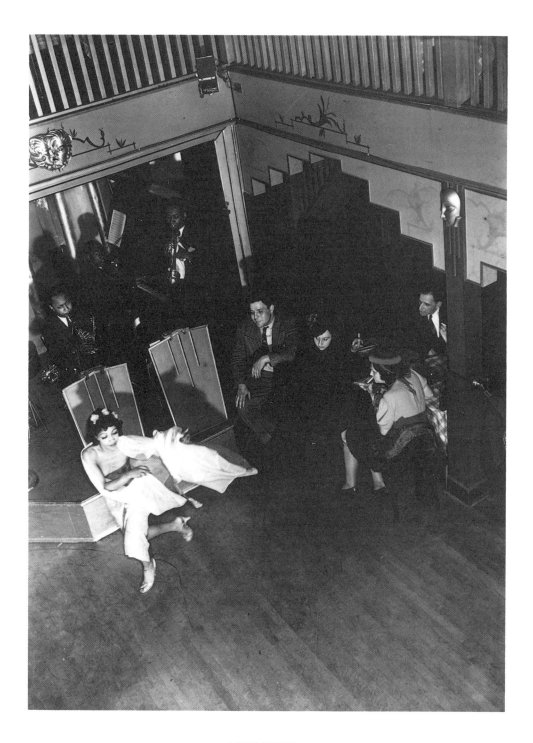

AARON SISKIND
(AMERICAN, 1903–1991)
Harlem c. 1937 Nightclub I, c. 1937
GELATIN SILVER PRINT, 1989.193.17
GIFT OF DR. DARYOUSH HOUSHMAND

80

The choice of subjects for the finials of the teapot and sugar bowl of this extremely rare service may seem to the modern viewer to espouse stereotypical racial thinking. To the nineteenth-century viewer, however, these motifs had less overt social implications. Iconographically, the most prominent figure on each vessel—an Oriental head on the teapot, an African sugarcane-picker on the sugar bowl, and a goat on the creamer—connote the contents. Certainly, though, the Asian and African details generally express imperialistic attitudes in late nineteenth-century America.

Their patterns of political, economic, and artistic behavior were forgotten—even the languages they had spoken in Africa. Like the poor whites of the South, they gathered together instead for fervent Christian revivalist camp meetings: they sang the hymns the poor whites sang, and if they sang them better and invented countless variations of great poignancy, nevertheless the old forms which they had achieved in Africa were forgotten. Conditions of slavery in America were so drastic that this loss is not to be wondered at. The slaves in any one plantation had come from tribes speaking mutually unintelligible languages, and with mutually unfamiliar arts of life; they had been herded together like cattle in slave ships and sold at the block in a strange and frightening world. They were worked hard on the plantations. It is no wonder that their owners remarked on their lack of any cultural achievements; the mistake they made was to interpret the degradation of the slave trade as if it were an innate and all-time characteristic of the American Negro. The Negro race has proud cultural achievements; not for very good reasons they were not spread before our eyes in America.

RUTH BENEDICT,
Race: Science and Politics

America and Europe
CHELSEA PORCELAIN MANUFACTORY (1745–1784)
LONDON, ENGLAND, 1758–1759
PORCELAIN, 60.12.54
BEQUEST OF JAMES HAZEN HYDE

Africa and Asia
CHELSEA PORCELAIN MANUFACTORY (1745–1784)
LONDON, ENGLAND, 1758–1759
PORCELAIN, 60.12.55
BEQUEST OF JAMES HAZEN HYDE

ANDY WARHOL
(AMERICAN, 1930–1987)
Untitled (from Ten Works—Ten Painters), 1964
SERIGRAPH, 86.285.9
GIFT OF R. WALLACE BOWMAN AND
RUTH BOWMAN

THOMAS HOVENDEN
(AMERICAN, 1840–1895)
Ain't That Ripe?, N.D.
OIL ON CANVAS, 32.825
GIFT OF THE EXECUTORS OF THE ESTATE
OF MICHAEL FRIEDSAM

FRANCIS WILLIAM EDMONDS
(AMERICAN, 1806–1863)
All Talk and No Work, 1855–1856
OIL ON CANVAS, 51.108
CARLL H. DE SILVER FUND

…the Prophet is reported to have said that those who will be most severely punished by God on the Day of Judgement will be the painters.

SIR THOMAS W. ARNOLD,
Painting in Islam

Arabic Phrase in Thulth Script
SIGNED: ISMAIL EFFENDI KATIB AYA-SOFIA-AL-KABIR
TURKEY, DATED 1198 A.H. (1783 A.D.)
INK ON PAPER GLUED TO WOODEN BOARD, X732
MUSEUM COLLECTION

The inscription reads: "My intercession is for those of my community who have committed great sins."

In the formation of Muslim dogma the Traditions of the Prophet have not been of less importance than the Qur'an itself: they are held by Muslim theologians to proceed from divine inspiration, though unlike the Qur'an, which is the eternal, uncreated Word of God, they are held to be inspired only as to content and meaning, but not in respect of actual verbal expression. Accordingly the Traditions enjoy an authority commensurate with that of the precepts of the Qur'an itself and are equally binding on the consciences of the faithful. On the subject of painting the Traditions are uncompromising in their condemnation and speak with no uncertain voice, e.g., the Prophet is reported to have said that those who will be most severely punished by God on the Day of Judgement will be the painters. On the Day of Judgement the punishment of hell will be meted out to the painter, and he will be called upon to breathe life into the forms that he has fashioned; but he cannot breathe life into anything. The reason for this damnation is this: in fashioning the form of a being that has life, the painter is usurping the creative function of the Creator and thus is attempting to assimilate himself to God; and the futility of the painter's claim will be brought home to him, when he will be made to recognize the ineffectual character of his creative activity, through his inability to complete the work of creation by breathing into the objects of his art, which look so much like living beings, the breath of life. The blasphemous character of his attempt is further emphasized by the use in this Tradition of the actual words of the Qur'an (v. 110) in which God describes the miraculous activity of Jesus—"Thou didst fashion of clay as it were the figure of a bird, by My permission, and didst breathe into it, and by My permission it became a bird." The making of forms by the painter could only be justified if he possessed such miraculous power as was given by God to His divinely inspired Prophet, Jesus, the Word of God.

The Arabic word for "painter," which has passed from Arabic into Persian, Turkish, and Urdu in the same sense, is 'musawwir', which literally means "forming, fashioning, giving form," and so can equally apply to the sculptor. The blasphemy in the appellation is the more apparent to the Muslim mind, in that this word is applied to God Himself in the Qur'an (LIX. 24): "He is god, the Creator, the Maker, the Fashioner" (musawwir). Thus the highest term of praise which in the Christian world can be bestowed upon the artist, in calling him a creator, in the Muslim world serves to emphasize the most damning evidence of his guilt.

SIR THOMAS W. ARNOLD,
Painting in Islam

85

MUHAMMAD IBN SULAYMAN FUZULI BAGHDADI
(C. 1480–1556)
SCRIBE: 'ASIZ ALLAH AL HUSAYNY AL-KASHANY
IRAQ, BAGHDAD, 1101 A.H. (DECEMBER 12, 1602)
The Prophet Muhammad in the Mosque with Companions, FOLIO
73A FROM THE *Hadiqa al Su'ada (Garden of Delight)*
BOUND MANUSCRIPT; WATERCOLORS, GOLD, AND
INK ON PAPER, 70.143
GIFT OF MR. AND MRS. CHARLES K. WILKINSON

The Prophet Muhammad is shown seated on a *minbar* or pulpit, with his face veiled and surrounded by a fiery nimbus. To either side are the angel Gabriel and the Prophet's son-in-law, 'Ali, cradling in his lap his sons Hasan and Husayn, also surrounded by nimbuses. Additionally, the Prophet and his grandsons wear the green turban identified with the Holy Family.

Western audiences and critics have traditionally perceived devotional painting as a rarity in Islamic art because of the prohibition against idolatry in the holy *Qur'an.* This prohibition was thought to extend to representational art of any sort, particularly in a religious context. Nevertheless, the Muslim attitude toward religious art varied considerably, and Muslim artists were depicting representational scenes for the decoration of royal palaces as early as the eighth century and illustrating manuscripts by the eleventh. Eventually, an acceptable form of depicting events from the history of early Islam and from the life of the Prophet in a textual context became necessary. At times, Muhammad was portrayed naturalistically, at times symbolically—as a flame, for instance. In some cases, extremely devout patrons or artists erased his features from illustrated manuscripts.

By the sixteenth century, illustrated devotional texts had become commonplace in the Ottoman and Safavid empires (Turkey and Persia). To circumvent orthodox restrictions, the painter of this manuscript—which was produced in Baghdad, then part of the Ottoman domain—has chosen to show the Prophet Muhammad but to hide his features under a veil, thus reaching a compromise between artistic integrity and established religious dogma.

86

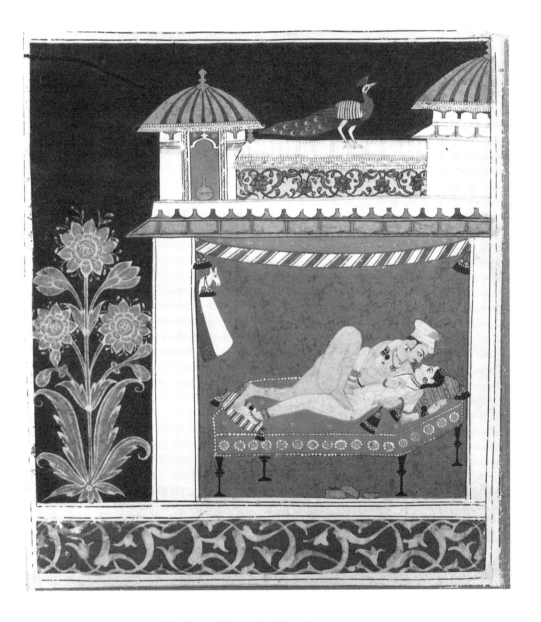

Folio from an Unidentified Manuscript, ANONYMOUS
CENTRAL INDIA, MALWA, C. 1680
OPAQUE WATERCOLOR ON PAPER, 84.201.3
ANONYMOUS GIFT

This painting shares many characteristics in common with illustrations to the *Amaru-sataka*, one hundred verses on love and its various moods, painted at Mewar, a principality in Rajasthan. Here, the page is not inscribed with any identifying text.

Sooner or later we shall have to get down to the humble task of exploring the depths of our consciousness and dragging to the light what sincere bits of reflected experience we can find. These bits will not always be beautiful, they will not always be pleasing, but they will be genuine.

EDWARD SAPIR,
"CULTURE, GENUINE AND SPURIOUS"

Mercury in Repose
NINETEENTH-CENTURY CAST FROM ROMAN BRONZE
IN THE NAPLES MUSEUM
BRONZE ON MARBLE BASE, 98.16
GIFT OF THE HON. EUGENE BLACKFORD

88

One should add that the natives' response to the first Europeans, insofar as it is recorded, provides evidence of a comparable reaction: one Amerindian, astonished at the French custom of collecting and carrying about mucus in handkerchiefs, wryly declared: "If thou likest that filth, give me thy handkerchief and I will soon fill it."

STEPHEN GREENBLATT,
"FILTHY RITES"

AUGUSTE RODIN
(FRENCH, 1840–1917)
The Age of Bronze, LARGE REDUCTION, 1876
(REDUCTION PROBABLY 1903), CAST 1967
BRONZE, 68.49
GIFT OF B. GERALD CANTOR

EGON SCHIELE
(AUSTRIAN, 1890–1918)
Male Nude (Self-Portrait I), 1912
LITHOGRAPH, X625.3
MUSEUM COLLECTION

Torso of a Roman Youth as Apollo
SECOND-CENTURY A.D. ROMAN COPY OF A TYPE
FREQUENTLY ENCOUNTERED IN THE SCULPTURAL
REPERTOIRE OF THE FOURTH CENTURY B.C.
WHITE MARBLE
PROVENANCE NOT KNOWN, 76.171
GIFT OF JULIUS J. IVANITSKY IN MEMORY OF HIS
PARENTS, IDA AND JACOB EVENITSKY.

As heirs to the cultural legacy of the ancient
Greeks, the Romans incorporated several Greek
cultural norms into the fabric of their civilization.
Notable was the Roman appropriation of the god
Apollo, whom Augustus, the first emperor of
Rome in the first century B.C., purposefully
selected as his tutelary deity. The choice was conscious because Apollo, the god of reason, symbol-
ized for the classical world the principle of a
sound mind in a sound body. To be cast in the
image of Apollo, therefore, was to be presented as
the embodiment of sobriety and physical fitness.
So it was, apparently, that the individuals com-
missioning this statue of an advantaged youth
desired to indicate that he too was sound of mind
and body. The use of the cape worn over the
shoulders provides a perfect foil against which to
regard the ideal forms of the body. The now miss-
ing head is thought to have been a representation
of the young man.

...when Malinowski ventured to suggest to the Trobriand islanders that they should discipline recalcitrant children by beating them, the islanders considered the idea "unnatural and immoral."

STEPHEN GREENBLATT
"FILTHY RITES"

JOHN KOCH
(AMERICAN, 1909–1978)
The Sculptor, 1964
OIL ON CANVAS, 69.165
GIFT OF THE ARTIST

ROBERT MAPPLETHORPE
(AMERICAN, 1946–1989)
Male Nude, 1982
GELATIN SILVER PRINT, 89.30.11
GIFT IN MEMORY OF JACK BOULTON

92

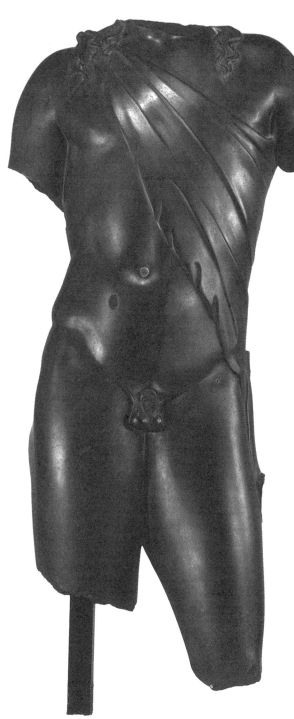

Torso of Dionysos, God of Wine and the Revel
SECOND-CENTURY A.D. ROMAN COPY OF A GREEK
ORIGINAL OF THE FOURTH CENTURY B.C.
BASALT
PROVENANCE NOT KNOWN, 80.249
GIFT OF MR. CHRISTIAN HUMANN

The civilization of ancient Greece and, to a degree, that of ancient Rome regarded the male body as a primary vehicle through which cultural ideals were made manifest. This is not to say, however, that each classical nude torso imparted the same message. This image was regarded as the visual expression of the cultural ideal of a sound mind in a sound body. When either mind or body was subjected to excess, an imbalance would be produced that might be deleterious to society. In selecting the image of Dionysos, the Greeks were making a statement that one's abrogation of reason as the result of an outside stimulus, wine in this case, allows passion to rule. And since passion is the realm of the beasts, ordered society suffers. Artistically these various elements are given expression by the attribute of the skin of a recently slain fawn worn as a shawl over the god's shoulder. Moreover, connoisseurs of Greek art will agree that the subtle, plump quality in the torso modeling of Dionysos' body is a direct reference to the weakening of the physique by sybaritic pursuits.

ROBIN SCHWARTZ
(AMERICAN, B. 1957)
Pete (FROM *Monkey Portrait Series*), 1988
GELATIN SILVER PRINT, 1989.141
CARLL H. DE SILVER FUND

Pharaoh Before an Otter or an Ichneumon
LATE PERIOD, C. 664–30 B.C.
BRONZE
EGYPT, 76.105.2
CHARLES EDWIN WILBOUR MEMORIAL FUND

A possible interpretation of the figure of a king with his hand to his genitals is that he is shown in his role of "living image of Atum," the solar demiurge who began the Creation by masturbating. The rearing otter or ichneumon—the Egyptians could confound the two animals—may be viewed as a manifestation of Atum and/or the solar eye, destroyer of forces hostile to the solar creator and pharaoh.

94

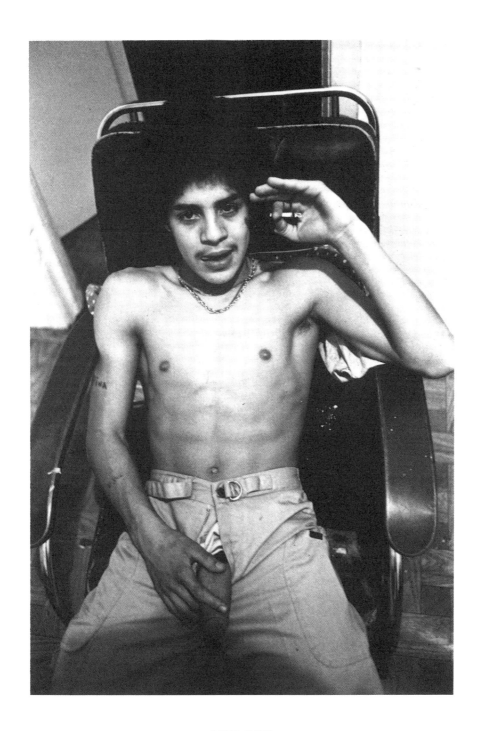

LARRY CLARK
(AMERICAN, B. 1953)
Exposed, 1981
GELATIN SILVER PRINT, 83.217.79
GIFT OF MARVIN SCHWARTZ

95

The question returns—when were these cover-ups perpetrated, these aggressions under the ægis of purity? We are not yet ready to produce a reliable periodization of Western prudishness in its subtler iconoclastic effects. But it does appear that resistance to the freedoms of art is diachronic. The virtuous disfigurement of so much Renaissance painting and sculpture cannot be blamed simply on recent Comstockery, or on Victorianism, or on 18th-century etiquette, or Calvinist Puritanism, or the bigotry that prevailed after the Council of Trent. The affront from which these successive ages recoiled was deep enough to have given offense in some quarters even while these works were created.

LEO STEINBERG,
*The Sexuality of Christ in Renaissance Art
and in Modern Oblivion*

WILLEM DE KOONING
(AMERICAN, B. 1904)
Untitled (Nude Woman), C. 1978
INK AND BRUSH WITH PENCIL, 84.306.1
GIFT OF MR. AND MRS. MORTON OSTOW

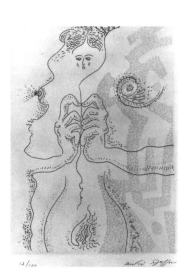

ANDRE MASSON
(FRENCH, B. 1896)
Le Fil d'Ariene NO. 6 (FROM THE
PORTFOLIO *For Meyer Schapiro*), 1973
ETCHING AND AQUATINT, 75.16.3
PRINT DEPARTMENT AUCTION FUND

96

WILLIAM GLACKENS
(AMERICAN, 1870–1938)
Nude with Apple, 1910
OIL ON CANVAS, 56.70
DICK S. RAMSAY FUND

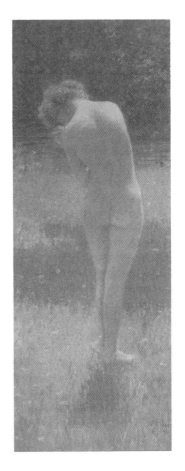

BOLTON COIT BROWN
(AMERICAN, 1865–1936)
Sifting Shadows, N.D.
OIL ON CANVAS, 17.135
GIFT OF QUILL JONES

BERNARD KARFIOL
(AMERICAN, 1886–1952)
The Awakening, N.D.
OIL ON CANVAS, 41.680
JOHN B. WOODWARD MEMORIAL FUND

97

HENRI MATISSE
(FRENCH, 1869–1954)
ILLUSTRATION FOR *L'Apres-Midi d'une Faune*
(FROM *Poeésies de Stéphane Mallarmé*), N.D.
ETCHING, 36.67.16
CARLL H. DE SILVER FUND

BEN KAMAHIRA
(AMERICAN, B. 1925)
The Mirror, N.D.
OIL ON CANVAS, 67.235
GIFT OF MR. AND MRS. JOHN KOCH

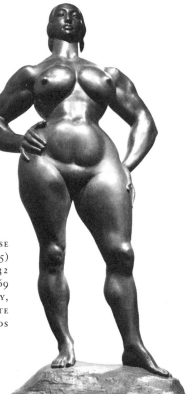

GASTON LACHAISE
(AMERICAN, 1882–1935)
Standing Woman, 1932
BRONZE, 56.69
FRANK S. BENSON, A. AUGUSTUS HEALY,
ALFRED T. WHITE
AND MUSEUM COLLECTION FUNDS

Granted that order spoils pattern; it also provides the materials of pattern. Order implies restriction; from all possible materials, a limited selection has been made and from all possible relations a limited set has been used. So disorder by implication is unlimited, no pattern has been realised in it, but its potential for patterning is indefinite. This is why, though we seek to create order, we do not simply condemn disorder. We recognise that it is destructive to existing patterns; also that it has potentiality. It symbolises both danger and power.

MARY DOUGLAS,
Purity and Danger

WILLIAM JACOB BAER
(AMERICAN, 1860–1941)
Daphne, 1911
OIL ON CANVAS, 11.523
GIFT OF WILLIAM A. PUTNAM AND WALTER H. CRITTENDEN

CIRCLE OF FRANÇOIS BOUCHER
(FRENCH, 1703–1770)
COPY OF *The Sleeping Bacchantes*, AFTER 1758
OIL ON CANVAS, 98.10
GIFT OF JAMES A. BELL

WILLEM DE KOONING
(AMERICAN, B. 1904)
Woman, 1953–1954
OIL ON PAPER, 57.124
GIFT OF MR. AND
MRS. ALASTAIR BRADLEY MARTIN

PHILIP EVERGOOD
(AMERICAN, 1901–1973)
The Tooters, 1961
OIL ON CANVAS, 62.76
GIFT OF THE FORD FOUNDATION

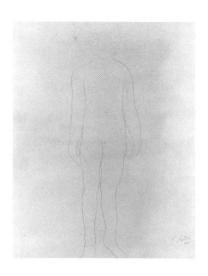

AUGUSTE RODIN
(FRENCH, 1840–1917)
Mademoiselle Jean, Standing, 1903
PENCIL, 87.94.2
GIFT OF THE B. GERALD CANTOR
ART FOUNDATION

AUGUSTE RODIN
(FRENCH, 1840–1917)
Bacchantes Embracing, BY 1905
BRONZE
NUMBER OF CAST/EDITION: VII/12, 84.77.2
GIFT OF IRIS AND B. GERALD CANTOR

In *Bacchantes Embracing*, Rodin addresses the theme of lesbian love. Apparently fascinated by this subject, he executed more than half a dozen groups of female lovers, including *Damned Women*. Although it is not known when this work was titled or by whom, the allusion to pagan mythology would have made the subject acceptable to Rodin's audience. The public tolerated such aberrant behavior in high art when it was distanced by a mythological title, but was scandalized when it possessed a non-specific immediacy indicated by such titles as *The Bathers*. At any rate, at least one of the women here appears not to be a follower of Bacchus at all but rather a female faun, identified by her goatlike furry legs and cloven hooves.

> "I found pictures at the exhibition that are simply lewd and others that are lewd only to artists."

MILTON BROWN,
The Story of the Armory Show

AUGUSTE RODIN
(FRENCH, 1840–1917)
The Sirens, 1880s, CAST 1967
BRONZE, NUMBER OF CAST/EDITION: V/12, 86.87.1
GIFT OF THE B. GERALD CANTOR ART FOUNDATION

AUGUSTE RODIN
(FRENCH, 1840–1917)
Damned Women, 1885–1911, CAST 1979
BRONZE, NUMBER OF CAST/EDITION: VII/12, 86.87.4
GIFT OF THE B. GERALD CANTOR ART FOUNDATION

While the confusing flurry of limbs makes it somewhat difficult to decipher the work, it is in fact a depiction of two women making love. Carrying realism to an extreme, Rodin is said to have employed as models a pair of lesbians who worked as professional dancers. By emphasizing motion and eroticism, he created a powerful image of the women. The projection of appendages into space convey a sense of excited movement. The arms of the reclining figure are raised above her head and rest on the rock in a gesture of surrender while the flexed muscles of her parted legs connote sexual ecstasy. The aggressor rests her right knee on the pubes of her partner and buries her face in her neck.

Lesbian lovers were a popular subject among Realists writers and artists, who were fascinated by aspects of life considered unacceptable for treatment by high art. Given Rodin's profound interest in both feminine beauty and eroticism, it is not surprising that he undertook this subject.

AUGUSTE RODIN
(FRENCH, 1840–1917)
Bacchantes Embracing, SMALL VERSION, BY 1900,
DATE OF CAST UNKNOWN
BRONZE
NUMBER OF CAST/EDITION: IV/12, 84.77.3
GIFT OF IRIS AND B. GERALD CANTOR

Brahmanical Triad
KASHMIR, EIGHTH CENTURY
GREEN CHLORITE, 78.209
A. AUGUSTUS HEALY FUND AND DESIGNATED
PURCHASE FUND

This unusual Kashmiri relief is concerned with the three principal deities of Brahmanism: at the center, a linga, the phallic emblem of Shiva, is flanked by two anthropomorphic deities Vishnu and Brahma. Shiva is generally understood to be the Destroyer, but the *linga* represents his potent procreative aspect.

EGYPT, SAID TO BE FROM ALEXANDRIA
Symplegma OR *A Group of Intertwined Figures*
(PTOLEMAIC PERIOD, 305–30 B.C.)
LIMESTONE, 58.13
CHARLES EDWIN WILBOUR MEMORIAL FUND

The concept of cyclic renewal—whether couched in religious terms such as the resurrection of the deceased in the Hereafter, in cosmic terms such as the rising of the sun on the morrow, or in political terms such as the orderly dynastic succession of pharaohs, or kings—was made manifest in Egyptian art by utilizing the model of human procreation. Thus this image, which to the uninformed appears to smack of the prurient aspects of group sex, is actually an allegory. The large male figure is a *sem*-priest, specifically charged with administering rites of passage from death to rebirth. This interpretation is reinforced not only by his puerile figure but also by his graphic union with the female, here the procreative principle. He is assisted by acolytes, two of whom subdue a bound oryx, a deerlike creature, symbolic of the Typhonic forces of chaos. As an allegory, then, this image can be understood as follows: Rites of passage, like human procreation, are critical and fraught with dangers. Necessary precautions must be observed, numerous individuals with specified roles must be engaged, and every opportunity to ensure safety against disorder must be entertained. The entire complex of human procreation from inception to delivery thereby becomes an eloquent analogy applicable equally to other aspects of ancient Egypt's polyvalent culture.

Intoxicated Ascetics
INDIA, PROVINCIAL MUGHAL, OUDH, C. 1775
OPAQUE WATERCOLOR AND GOLD ON PAPER, 84.183
ANONYMOUS GIFT

This painting is problematic. It is a pastiche of Muslim themes modeled on the works of Mir Kalan Khan, a prominent artist at Oudh in eastern India, who is mostly known through later copies of his style. The scenes, taken from Muslim literary sources, include Rustam lassoing Kabus (lower left) and hunters identified as Khord Salim Mirza Javan-Bakht and Shah 'Alam Padshah, who are perhaps Aurangzeb and one of his princes (lower right). The lady in a howdah may be one of the heroines of the Persian poet Nizami (upper right) and the elephant combat (top center) may be taken from a model in the Akbar nama. At the center, various stages in hashish (bhang) or opium-eating rituals are illustrated and two figures are engaged in an act that may be an antinomian practice said to be part of ascetic ritual.

There is a wide range of opinion among scholars about the content of the painting, including the religious identity of the figures. Clearly it is idiosyncratic, and not a common subject matter. Although the central figures seem to be ascetics, whether they are Hindu or Muslim is unclear.

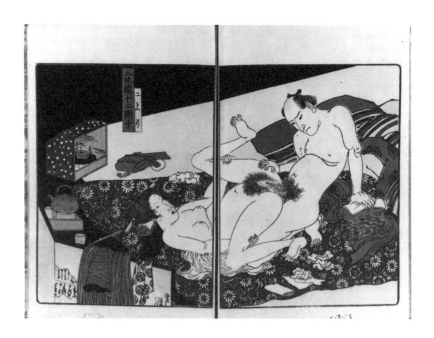

'ISODA KORYŪ SAI
(JAPANESE, ACTIVE 1766–1788)
ILLUSTRATION FROM
AN UNIDENTIFIED *shunga* ALBUM
JAPAN, EDO PERIOD, EIGHTEENTH CENTURY
WOODBLOCK PRINT, 78.141
GIFT OF WILLIAM E. HARKINS

To the traditional Japanese, sex represented neither a romantic ideal nor a phallic rite of the gods; it was simply the joyful union of the sexes and a natural function. Shunga were thus considered a normal subject for the Japanese artist, no more improper or degrading than the painting of a nude or a classical love scene seemed to a contemporary Western artist.

RICHARD LANE,
Kodansha Encyclopedia of Japan

CHŌ BUNSAI EISHI
(JAPANESE, 1754–1806)
DOUBLE-PAGE ILLUSTRATION FROM A *shunga* SERIES,
Hano no Ikkyō sho
JAPAN, EDO PERIOD, NINETEENTH CENTURY
WOODBLOCK PRINT, 82.230
GIFT OF EDWARD P. WEINMAN

YANAGAWA SHIGENOBU
(JAPANESE, 1787–1832)
ILLUSTRATION FROM THE *Shamisen Junichoshi*
JAPAN, EDO PERIOD, C. 1820, 80.177.4A
GIFT OF JACK HENTEL

The tradition of shunga, or "spring pictures," printed handbooks of explicit sex, dates to the late seventeenth century in Japan and was part of the genre celebrating the pleasure quarters of Edo.

As soon as the photographic image is seen as too threatening it does not qualify as art; nor is it perceived as such. Its threat is too plain. Then, of course, it can be censored—or kept under covers, or appropriately, in the bedroom, and certainly away from children and old maids—it *must* be censored. We begin to come closer to the relationship between realism and censorship. What is realistic is ugly and vulgar. Art is beautiful and high. The photograph is realistic; it is vulgar; it elicits natural and realistic responses. In art, nudity is beautiful and ideal; in the photograph (unless it has acquired the status of art), it is ugly and (therefore?) provocative.

DAVID FREEDBERG,
The Power of Images

LARRY CLARK
(AMERICAN, B. 1953)
Since I Became a Photographer, 1981
GELATIN SILVER PRINT, 83.217.41
GIFT OF MARVIN SCHWARTZ

LARRY CLARK
(AMERICAN, B. 1953)
In the Back Seat, 1981
GELATIN SILVER PRINT, 83.217.43
GIFT OF MARVIN SCHWARTZ

LARRY CLARK
(AMERICAN, B. 1953)
Trio, Boy with Hat on, 1981
GELATIN SILVER PRINT, 83.217.82
GIFT OF MARVIN SCHWARTZ

Arousal by image (whether pornographic or not) only occurs in context: in the context of the individual beholder's conditioning, and, as it were, of his preparation for seeing the arousing, erotic, or pornographic image. It is dependent on the prior availability of images and prevailing boundaries of shame. If one has not seen too many images of a particular kind before, and if the particular image infringes some preconception of what should not be or is not usually exposed (to the gaze), then the image may well turn out to be arousing.

DAVID FREEDBERG,
The Power of Images

LARRY CLARK
(AMERICAN, B. 1953)
Blowjob, 1981
GELATIN SILVER PRINT, 83.217.44
GIFT OF MARVIN SCHWARTZ

LARRY CLARK
(AMERICAN, B. 1953)
On a Blanket, 1981
GELATIN SILVER PRINT, 83.217.42
GIFT OF MARVIN SCHWARTZ

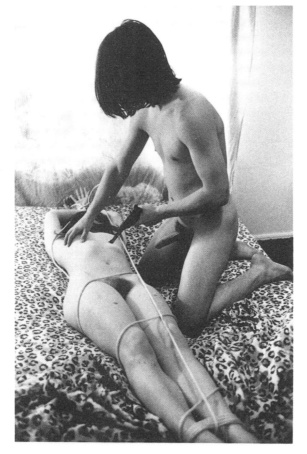

LARRY CLARK
(AMERICAN, B. 1953)
Brother and Sister, 1981
GELATIN SILVER PRINT, 83.217.45
GIFT OF MARVIN SCHWARTZ

III

Kendall and the artist Albert Herter became friends at the Art Students League. It was a fruitful friendship for Kendall, resulting in a number of portrait commissions from members of the prominent Herter family. In 1904 Herter's niece Christine, then thirteen, began taking private painting lessons from Kendall. They shared a common interest in playing the violin and a friendship developed quickly between them. For years Christine was almost a daily visitor to Kendall's studio, first in New York City and then in Tarrytown, and when Kendall moved to Newport she followed and rented a studio nearby. When she travelled to Europe, as she did most summers, she and Kendall wrote constantly.

About the time Kendall joined Yale, Christine left for Paris to continue her studies. When she returned, shortly after war was declared in Europe, she enrolled at Yale as a student in the fine arts department, but continued to work in Kendall's studio, occasionally posing for him....

Americans have never felt entirely comfortable with paintings of the nude. Perhaps Kendall's nudes were so well liked because they showed children and were therefore removed from a sexual context.

ROBERT AUSTIN,
"WILLIAM SERGEANT KENDALL, PAINTER OF CHILDREN"

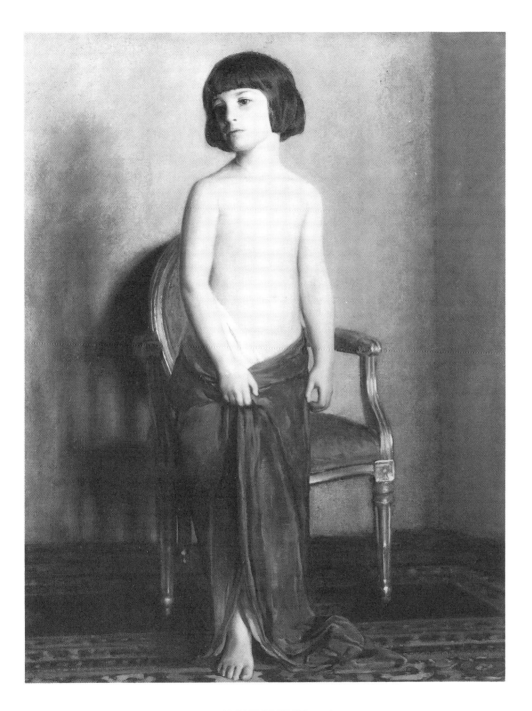

WILLIAM SERGEANT KENDALL
(AMERICAN, 1869–1938)
A Statuette, 1915
OIL ON CANVAS, 45.165
GIFT OF MRS. WILLIAM SERGEANT KENDALL

From the pictures sent in for the exhibition it is clear that the eye of some men shows them things otherwise than as they are—that there really are men who on principle feel meadows to be blue, the heaven green, clouds sulphur-yellow—or as they perhaps prefer to say "experience" them thus. I need not ask whether they really do see or feel things in this way, but in the name of the German people I have only to prevent these pitiable unfortunates who clearly suffer from defects of vision from attempting with violence to persuade contemporaries by their chatter that these faults of observation are indeed realities or from presenting them as "Art." Here only two possibilities are open: either these "artists" do really see things in this way and believe in that which they represent—then one has but to ask how the defect in vision arose, and if it is hereditary the Minister of the Interior will have to see to it that so ghastly a defect of the vision shall not be allowed to perpetuate itself—or if they do *not* believe in the reality if such impressions but seek on other grounds to impose upon the nation by this humbug, then it is a matter for a criminal court.

ADOLF HITLER

The artist does not create for the artist: he creates for the people and we will see to it that henceforth the people will be called in to judge its art.

ADOLF HITLER

ROBERT MAPPLETHORPE
(AMERICAN, 1946–1989)
Calla Lily, 1984
MANUFACTURED BY SWID POWELL
NEW YORK, 1989
PORCELAIN, 1990.34.4
GIFT OF SWID POWELL

ROBERT MAPPLETHORPE
(AMERICAN, 1946–1989)
Flower, 1986
MANUFACTURED BY SWID POWELL
NEW YORK, 1989
PORCELAIN, 1990.34.5
GIFT OF SWID POWELL

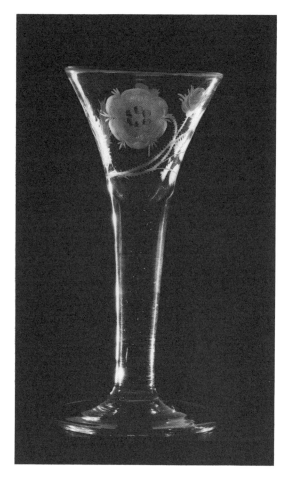

Wineglass
ENGLAND, C. 1745–1750
COLORLESS LEAD GLASS
WITH ETCHED DECORATION, 13.740
SPECIAL SUBSCRIPTION AND COLLECTION FUND

Wineglass
ENGLAND, C. 1730–1740
COLORLESS LEAD GLASS
WITH ETCHED DECORATION, 13.535
SPECIAL SUBSCRIPTION AND COLLECTION FUND

It is highly unusual for sophisticated decorative arts objects to espouse overt political meaning. Among the most fascinating of these rare objects are eighteenth-century English wineglasses with political engraving. These glasses are divided into two camps: Williamite and Jacobite. Williamite glassware marks the ascension in 1688 of William III (1650-1702), Prince of Orange, to the English throne. These glasses are engraved with equestrian or bust portraits of William, emblems such as the orange tree, and slogans that commemorate the Protestant victory over James II at the Battle of Boyne in 1690. Jacobite glassware champions the opposing clandestine Catholic cause of James II and his descendants, James Edward Stuart, the "Old Pretender," and his son Charles Edward Stuart, Bonnie Prince Charles the "Young Pretender." Typical Jacobite motifs include portraits of the Pretenders; the English rose and one or two buds; the Scottish thistle; a star; an oak leaf; and slogans such as *"Fiat"* (Let It Be Done), *"Redeat"* (May He Return), and *"Audentior Ibo"* (I Will Go More Boldly).

116

The people when it passes through these galleries will recognize in me its own spokesman and counselor: it will draw a sigh of relief and express its glad agreement with this purification of art. And that is decisive: an art which cannot count on the readiest and most intimate agreement of the great mass of the people, an art which must rely upon the support of small cliques, is intolerable. Such an art does but endeavor to confuse, instead of gladly reinforcing, the sure and healthy instinct of the people. The artist cannot stand aloof from his people. This exhibition is but a beginning, yet the end of the artistic stultification of Germany has begun. Now is the opportunity for youth to start its industrious apprenticeship, and when a sacred conscientiousness at last comes into its own, then I doubt not that the Almighty, from the mass of these decent creators of art, will once more raise up individuals to the eternal starry heaven of the imperishable god-favored artists of the great periods.

ADOLF HITLER

KARL L. H. MULLER
(AMERICAN, B. GERMANY, 1820–1887)
Pitcher
MANUFACTURED BY UNION PORCELAIN WORKS
(1863–C. 1922), BROOKLYN, 1876
PORCELAIN, 68.87.51
GIFT OF FRANKLIN CHACE

117

The condition under which the Gestapo allowed the
Bauhaus to continue its work were far too rigorous
for the members of the faculty to be induced to withdraw
their statement of dissolution; the fact that they
would have been accepted had not the dissolution been
already decided on, was later claimed solely for reasons
of security.

Strictly Confidential
State Secret police
Berlin S.W. 11, July 21, 1933
Prinz-Albrecht-Strasse 8
Professor Mies van der Rohe
Berlin, Am Karlsbad 24
Regarding: Bauhaus Berlin-Steglitz

In agreement with the Prussian Minister of Science, Art and Education, the
reopening of the Bauhaus Berlin-Steglitz is made dependent upon the removal
of some objections.

1) Ludwig Hilberseimer and Vassily Kandinsky are no longer permitted to teach.
   Their places have to be taken by individuals who guarantee to support the
   principles of the National Socialist ideology.
2) The curriculum which has been in force up to now is not sufficient to satisfy the
   demands of the new State for the purposes of building its inner structure.
   Therefore, a curriculum accordingly modified is to be submitted to the
   Prussian Minister of Culture.
3) The members of the faculty have to complete and submit a questionnaire,
   satisfying the requirements of the civil service law.

The decision on the continuing existence and the reopening of the Bauhaus will be
made dependent on the immediate removal of the objections and fulfillment of the
stated conditions.

By order: (signed) Dr. Peche
Attested: (illegible)
chancery staff

Behind the specific accusations which were made against the new architecture in Weimar there lay a vaguer yet more disquieting sentiment: the fear that iconoclasm in the arts must extend its effects to broader realms of the cultural and social order, disturbing, in the end, all established traditions.

BARBARA LANE MILLER,
Architecture and Politics in Germany, 1918 to 1945

MARCEL BREUER
(AMERICAN, B. HUNGARY, 1902–1981)
Coffee Table B19
MANUFACTURED BY THONET BROTHERS, VIENNA, AUSTRIA, 1928
CHROMIUM-PLATED TUBULAR STEEL, GLASS, AND RUBBER, 59.236.5
GIFT OF MR. AND MRS. ALEXIS ZALSTEM-ZALESSKY

No one must say that the people has no understanding for a really valuable enrichment of its cultural life. Before the critics did justice to the genius of a Richard Wagner he had the people on his side, while the people has had nothing to do with so-called "modern art." The people regarded this art as the outcome of an impudent and unashamed arrogance or of a simply shocking lack of skill; it felt that this art-stammer—these achievements which might have been produced by untalented children of from eight to ten years old—could never be valued as an expression of our own times or of the German future.

ADOLF HITLER

MARCEL BREUER
(AMERICAN, B. HUNGARY, 1902–1981)
Side Chair B5, 1926–1927
MANUFACTURED BY THONET BROTHERS, VIENNA, AUSTRIA, C. 1929–1931
CHROMIUM-PLATED TUBULAR STEEL AND CANVAS, 59.236.2
GIFT OF MR. AND MRS. ALEXIS ZALSTEM-ZALESSKY

The Exhibitions and publications of the Bauhaus represent decadent values which the leadership and masters of the Bauhaus inflate theatrically into "art."…. It is presumption to declare that the state sins against culture by withdrawing its support and friendship from this institute. The bloodless and sick art instinct and empty science…which up to now have been supported by the heads of state and by those of its branches which are responsible for the cultural development of the state, do not maintain and further our culture. They further only decadence.

BARBARA LANE MILLER,
Architecture and Politics in Germany, 1918 to 1945

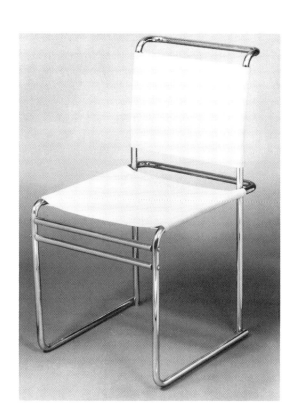

MARCEL BREUER
(AMERICAN, B. HUNGARY, 1902–1981)
Arm Chair B3, 1925
MANUFACTURED BY STANDARD-MOBEL
BERLIN, GERMANY, 1927–1928
CHROMIUM-PLATED TUBULAR STEEL
AND CANVAS, 59.236.4
GIFT OF MR. AND MRS. ALEXIS
ZALSTEM-ZALESSKY

FRANCISCO GOYA Y LUCIENTES
(SPANISH, 1746–1828)
Qual la descañonan!
(HOW THEY ARE PLUCKING HER!)
(PLATE 21 FROM *Los Caprichos*), 1792–1799
AQUATINT AND ETCHING, 68.192.45
GIFT OF MRS. EDWIN DE T. BECHTEL

Correccion (CORRECTION)
(PLATE 46 FROM *Los Caprichos*), 1792–1799
AQUATINT AND ETCHING, 38.781
GIFT OF J. B. NEUMANN

Al Conde Palatino
(TO THE COUNT PALATINE)
(PLATE 33 FROM *LosCaprichos*), 1792–1799
AQUATINT AND ETCHING, 68.192.46
GIFT OF MRS. EDWIN DE T. BECHTEL

Duendecitos (LITTLE GOBLINS)
(PLATE 49 FROM *Los Caprichos*), 1792–1799
AQUATINT AND ETCHING, 68.192.47
GIFT OF MRS. EDWIN DE T. BECHTEL

Miren que grabes.

Donde vá mama.

Devota profesion.

¿Está Umd ...pues, Como dígo. eh! Cuidado! si no!.

Miren que grabes! (LOOK HOW SERIOUS THEY ARE!)
(PLATE 63 FROM *Los Caprichos*), 1792–1799
AQUATINT AND ETCHING, 68.192.48
GIFT OF MRS. EDWIN DE T. BECHTEL

Devota profesion (DEVOUT VOWS)
(PLATE 70 FROM *Los Caprichos*), 1792–1799
AQUATINT AND ETCHING, 38.780
GIFT OF J. B. NEUMANN

Donde va mamá? (WHERE IS MAMA GOING?)
(PLATE 65 FROM *Los Caprichos*), 1792–1799
AQUATINT AND ETCHING, 68.192.49
GIFT OF MRS. EDWIN DE T. BECHTEL

Está Umd ...pues, Como dígo...eh! Cuidado! Si no!..
(YOUR HONOR IS...WELL...AS I SAY...EH!
BE CAREFUL...OTHERWISE!...)
(PLATE 76 FROM *Los Caprichos*), 1792–1799
AQUATINT AND ETCHING, 38.778
GIFT OF J. B. NEUMANN

HONORÉ DAUMIER
(FRENCH, 1808–1879)
Pique-Assiette (PLATE 9 FROM *Bohémiens de Paris*), 1941
LITHOGRAPH, 53.166.19
A. AUGUSTUS HEALY FUND

WILLIAM HOGARTH
(ENGLISH, 1697–1764)
The Reward of Cruelty (FROM *Four Stages of Cruelty*), 1751
ENGRAVING, 22.1874
BEQUEST OF SAMUEL E. HASLETT

PABLO PICASSO
(SPANISH, 1881–1973)
La Minotauromachie, 1935
ETCHING, 59.30
FRANK L. BABBOTT AND FREDERICK LOESER FUNDS

Goebbels Forbids Art Criticism

Because this year has not brought an improvement in art criticism, I forbid once and for all the continuance of art criticism in its past form, effective as of today [November 27, 1936]. From now on, the reporting of art will take the place of an art criticism which has set itself up as a judge of art— a complete perversion of the concept of "criticism" which dates from the time of the Jewish domination of art. The critic is to be superseded by the art editor. The reporting of art should not be concerned with values, but should confine itself to description. Such reporting should give the public a chance to make its own judgments, should stimulate it to form an opinion about artistic achievements through its own attitudes and feelings.

JOSEPH GOEBBELS

GEORGE GROSZ
(GERMAN, 1893–1959)
Die Kommunisten fallen—und die Devisen steigen
(THE COMMUNISTS FALL AND FOREIGN EXCHANGE RISES);
ALSO TITLED, *Ecrasez la famine–Blood is the Best Sauce*
(PLATE 3 FROM THE PORTFOLIO *Gott mit uns*), 1919
PHOTOTRANSFER LITHOGRAPH, 43.170.31
MUSEUM PURCHASE

125

LISA DOW AND SANDY   **"LIVING WITH AIDS"**   QUEENS, NY., NOVEMBER 5, 1987

TOM MCGOVERN
(AMERICAN, B. 1957)
Lisa Dow and Sandy, (FROM *Living with* AIDS), 1987
GELATIN SILVER PRINT , 1989.140.1A–C
CARLL H. DE SILVER FUND

СПАСИБО ТОВАРИЩУ СТАЛИНУ ЗА НАШЕ СЧАСТЛИВОЕ ДЕТСТВО!

VITALY KOMAR (AMERICAN, B. USSR 1943)
AND ALEXANDER MELAMID (AMERICAN, B. USSR 1945)
Thank You Comrade Stalin for Our Happy Childhood, 1983
SCREENPRINT, 85.128.1
GIFT OF DR. ANNE C. KOLKER

A few years ago, with this in mind, I proceeded to find out how we use the term free in the mid-twentieth century…. I came reluctantly to the conclusion that the term free was almost never used, except by people whose function it was to evoke or facilitate freedom, or to remind people about freedom, or to prod people into being concerned about it, that is, by people such as social scientists, politicians, psychoanalysts, and educators. Otherwise, the term free was not applied to the freedom of the self.

KURT WOLFF,
This Is the Time for Radical Anthropology

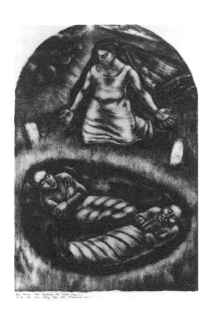

GEORGE BIDDLE
(AMERICAN, 1885–1959)
In Memoriam: Sacco and Vanzetti, 1930
LITHOGRAPH, 67.185.23
GIFT OF THE ARTIST

ROCKWELL KENT
(AMERICAN, 1882–1971)
August 23 (Sacco and Vanzetti), 1927
WOOD ENGRAVING, 56.4.25
GIFT OF ERHART WEYHE

Assassination is the extreme form of censorship.

GEORGE BERNARD SHAW

WANG ZHEN
(CHINESE, 1866–1938)
Blind Man and Dog, 1927
INK AND COLOR ON PAPER, 86.271.12
GIFT OF DR. AND MRS. JOHN LYDEN

A painter, calligrapher, and poet, Wang Zhen was interested in figural subjects, Buddhist images, and flower-and-bird painting. His work was popular in Japan, and he was employed for a time before the outbreak of World War II by a Japanese shipping company. However, when the war broke out, to assert his patriotism, he left his job and moved from occupied Shanghai to Hong Kong. In this painting, the artist depicts the image of a blind beggar to protest against a corrupt and snobbish society, as his inscription on the picture reads:

"This blind man has never been virtuous. He did bad things in his former life, therefore, he is being punished in his present life. He is roaming the streets with his cane and dog. He has not begged from farmers, workers, merchants; neither from the porters nor pedestrians. He has only begged from the officials and aristocrats. Do not laugh at him and think he is unimportant. He was formerly a high official. It is very sad that the human is in worse condition than the dog. The dog's faithfulness lasts longer than the human. If a man does not have money his relatives will stay away from him, but the dog is faithful to even the poor. The dog has virtues, but the human does not. Dog-dog-dog. Do not become attached to the wealthy. Do not bark at the poor people. You must remember the way of the world. The inconstancy of human relationship is the ugliest."

The people who assail images do so in order to make clear that they are not afraid of them, and thereby prove their fear. It is not simply fear of what is represented; it is fear of the object itself.

DAVID FREEDBERG,
The Power of Images

ARTIST UNKNOWN
(FRENCH, LATE FIFTEENTH CENTURY)
*Martyrdom of Saints Cosmas and Damian with Their
Three Brothers*, c. 1490
OIL ON PANEL, 32.840
GIFT OF THE EXECUTORS
OF THE ESTATE OF MICHAEL FRIEDSAM

Much Christian art suffered a period of violent iconoclasm in northern Europe during the Reformation of the sixteenth century. This painting, as can be seen from the photographic detail of the work before restoration, seems to have been subject to such attacks. The mouths have been marred with X's and the executioners's sleeve and the martyr's brocade robe show longer scratches. Reformation iconoclasts often centered their attacks on the faces, eyes, and mouths of the figures represented, and the systematic, purposeful mutilation of the mouths here suggests an attempt to silence the figures, to render them lifeless.

The mode of iconoclasm which is called censorship does not necessarily take the form of direct assault or removal. Its cunning consists in denying its own operation and leaving no scars.

LEO STEINBERG,
The Sexuality of Christ in Renaissance Art and in Modern Oblivion

NEW KINGDOM, DYNASTY XVIII,
REIGN OF AKHENATEN
EGYPT; FROM HERMOPOLIS, BUT ORIGINALLY
FROM AKHETATEN, MODERN EL AMARNA,
(C. 1352–1336 B.C.)
*Nefertiti, Chief Queen of Akhenaten,
Kissing Her Daughter Merit-Aten*
LIMESTONE, 60.197.8
CHARLES EDWIN WILBOUR MEMORIAL FUND

This block is probably from a temple relief of the royal couple and their daughters under an image of the god Aten as a sun-disk with rays ending in hands. The hand preserved offers a sign of "life" to the queen. Images of Akhenaten or Nefertiti kissing a daughter have been interpreted as symbols of transmission to the child of life, power and legitimacy of rule. More than one explanation is possible for the ancient attacks, on one or two occasions, on Nefertiti's face and on the inscription, where the "Merit" in "Merit-Aten" has been erased, and where Nefertiti's name may have been erased.

LORENZO DI NICCOLO
(ITALIAN, C. EARLY FIFTEENTH CENTURY)
St. Lawrence Rescues Souls from Purgatory, N.D.
TEMPERA AND GOLD ON PANEL, 03.75
GIFT OF A. AUGUSTUS HEALY

In many Renaissance paintings the figures of demons, like other tortures of Christ and the saints, have been defaced by the pious. Although this painting has been restored by the conservator's hand, the scratches on the devils are still visible.

Torso of Akhenaten
REIGN OF AKHENATEN, (C. 1347–1336 B.C.)
INDURATED LIMESTONE, FROM EL AMARNA;
FOUND ON THE SOUTHEAST SIDE OF THE GREAT TEMPLE BY
HOWARD CARTER AND W. M. F. PETRIE IN 1891–1892, 58.2
CHARLES EDWIN WILBOUR MEMORIAL FUND

Akhenaten filled the temples of the Aten temple at El Amarna with colossal statues of himself, carved in the unusual style that had been developed in the early years of his reign when he still lived at Thebes and called himself Amenhotep IV. These statues depict the king with a long sinewy neck, sharp collarbones, small soft breasts, and a shallow channel on the stomach leading to the navel. The surviving traces of the king's lower body on this fragmentary sculpture show that the hips were quite broad; on better preserved statues Akhenaten appears with a huge distended abdomen and protruding buttocks.

After Akhenaten fell from power, his image and those of his family and his god, the Aten, suffered from relentless mutilation. Traditional-minded Egyptians, who no doubt saw the Amarna Period as a time of heresy, set out to erase all memory of his reign. Cartouches with Aten's name were effaced and statues of the heretic king were pulled down and smashed.

Eakins' methods of instruction at the academy provided the starting point. His insistence that all students study from the human figure began to disturb the Philadelphia academy community during Eakins' tenure as Director of Instruction after 1879. Members of the academy board were anxious to make the instruction self-sustaining and were responsive to the occasional complaints of parents and of academy students that Eakins' rigid prescriptions were too inflexible for the casual student. A certain amount of sexual reserve dominated the public life of the community, giving for some critics a prurient cast to Eakins' matter-of-fact use of models of both sexes for students of both sexes. After increasing tension, in 1886 the board insisted that Eakins resign from his post. The action hurt Eakins deeply, for it was directed not only at him but at principles that he felt to be of unquestionable importance.

ELIZABETH JOHNS,
*Thomas Eakins: The Heroism of
Modern Life*

THOMAS EAKINS
(AMERICAN, 1844–1916)
William Rush Carving His Allegorical Figure of the Schuykill River, 1908
OIL ON CANVAS, 39.461
DICK S. RAMSAY FUND

DOTTY ATTIE
(AMERICAN, B. 1938)
Barred from the Studio, 1987
OIL ON CANVAS, 88.165A–F
GIFT OF CHERYL AND HENRY WELT

133

Carpenter (1971) reports in *TV Guide* that his own introduction of pictures in 1970 to people in New Guinea created vast changes in a short time. He reports that after the taking of pictures of a circumcision ritual, the people gave up the ritual and substituted pictures for it. He questions his own role in this matter and wonders if he himself had given enough thought to the change he unknowingly created. This change was created, not by teaching people to make and to control their own visual symbolic forms, but merely by showing them pictures he had taken. How much greater might the change have been had he introduced into that culture the ability to make their own movies?

SOL WORTH,
"TOWARD AN ANTHROPOLOGICAL
POLITICS OF SYMBOLISM"

CINDY SHERMAN
(AMERICAN, B. 1954)
Untitled, 1985
COLOR PHOTOGRAPH, 86.36
FRANK L. BABBOTT FUND AND
CHARLES S. SMITH MEMORIAL FUND

When the makers of Pepsi Cola moved into the Thai soft drink market, they began an advertising campaign with the American slogan, "Come alive, you're in the Pepsi generation." The company said it later realized that the Thai translation it was using said, "Pepsi brings your ancestors back from the dead."

THE NEW YORK TIMES

Figure
COCHITI, NEW MEXICO, NINETEENTH CENTURY
CERAMIC, SLIPS, 02.257.2473
MUSEUM PURCHASE

Zealously destroyed by the early Spanish missionaries and, until recently, largely ignored by contemporary scholars and collectors, Pueblo figurative ceramics have suffered a history of both censure and neglect. For the Indians themselves, however, pottery has remained an art form that has helped to maintain native traditions and to confront new cultural influences. This late nineteenth-century Cochiti figure, produced for a growing non-Indian market, illustrates the potter's critical and comical view of the whites. Figures such as this, described by the whites who purchased them as "primitive idols" and "eccentric grotesques," were in fact caricatures of the white man himself, mocking portraits of the artist's new patron.

135

If left unchecked, we and perhaps other nations like us will continue to sell the technology which produces visual symbolic forms, while at the same time teaching other peoples *our uses only*, our conceptions, our codes, our mythic and narrative forms. We will, with technology, enforce our notions of what is, what is important, and what is right. The questions that anthropologists have been struggling with (related to whether we as anthropologists should help the oppressed as well as the oppressor), whether we should take sides in the questions of culture change or even culture destruction, assume new dimensions when transformed from physical to symbolic forms. While answers are not simple in this area, should we not consider the question whether we who strive to learn about others should take some responsibility for helping others to learn about themselves? Should we not consider whether we have a responsibility, at the very least, to explain to those we study that new technologies of communication need not be used only in the ways of the technological societies that introduce them?

SOL WORTH,
"TOWARD AN ANTHROPOLOGICAL
POLITICS OF SYMBOLIC FORMS"

ANDRES LOPEZ AND ANTONIO DE VEGAS
(SPANISH, ACTIVE IN SEGOVIA 1505–1511)
Martyrdom of St. Agatha, EARLY SIXTEENTH CENTURY
OIL ON PANEL, 53.91
GIFT OF MRS. J. FULLER FEDER

137

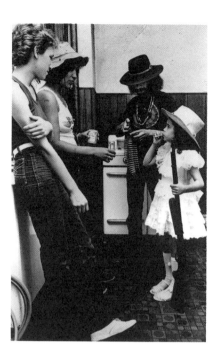

ATTRIBUTED TO JOHN GEORGE BROWN
(AMERICAN, 1831–1913)
Standing Boy Smoking a Cigar, 1867
OIL ON CANVAS, 32.802
GIFT OF THE EXECUTORS OF
THE ESTATE OF MICHAEL FRIEDSAM

STEVEN BAMBERG
(AMERICAN, TWENTIETH CENTURY)
The Baptism of Emily, 1980
GELATIN SILVER PRINT, 82.30.3
GIFT OF THE ARTIST

ANDRES SERRANO
(AMERICAN, B. 1950)
Caged Meat, 1983
CIBACHROME PRINT, 87.208
GIFT OF THE ARTIST

The sanguine life and terrifying aspects of primitive life, which civilized individuals could hardly sustain, precisely because of the immediate personal contexts in which they occur, do not begin to compete with increases in scope as civilization spreads and deepens.... Certain ritual dramas or aspects of them acknowledge, express, and symbolize the most destructive, ambivalent, and demoniacal aspects of human nature; in so doing, they are left limited and finite; that is, they become self-limiting. For this, as yet, we have no civilized parallel, no functional equivalent.

STANLEY DIAMOND,
"PRIMITIVE SOCIETY IN ITS
MANY DIMENSIONS"

Power Figure
(*Nyangboliafo*)
FON PEOPLES, PEOPLE'S REPUBLIC OF BENIN,
NINETEENTH OR TWENTIETH CENTURY
WOOD, BONES, SHELLS, FIBER,
AND SACRIFICIAL MATERIAL, 49.45
MUSEUM PURCHASE

To think deeply in our culture is to grow angry and to anger others; and if you cannot tolerate this anger, you are wasting the time you spend thinking deeply. One of he rewards of deep thought is the hot glow of anger at discovering a wrong, but if anger is taboo, thought will starve to death.

JULES HENRY
Culture against Man

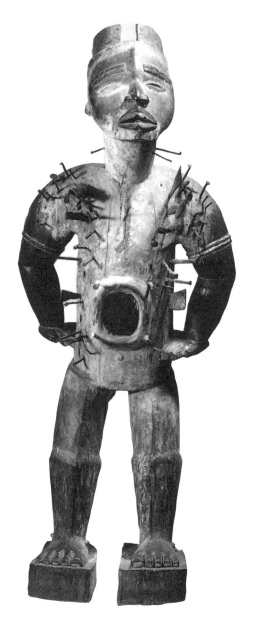

Power Figure
(Nkisi Nkondi)
YOMBE GROUP, KONGO PEOPLES, ZAIRE,
NINETEENTH CENTURY
WOOD, IRON, MIRROR, AND RESIN, 22.1421
MUSEUM PURCHASE

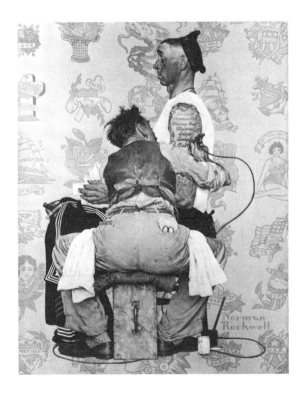

NORMAN ROCKWELL
(AMERICAN, 1894–1978)
The Tattoo Artist, 1944
OIL ON CANVAS, 69.8
GIFT OF THE ARTIST

LARRY CLARK
(AMERICAN, B. 1953)
First Time Shooting Up, 1981
GELATIN SILVER PRINT, 83.217.37
GIFT OF MARVIN SCHWARTZ

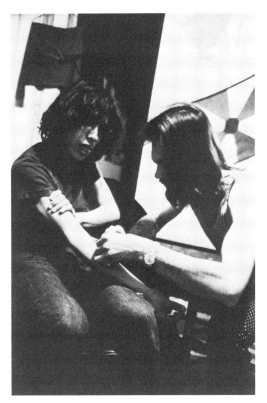

ROBERT BLUM
(AMERICAN, 1857–1903)
The Vintage Festival, 1896–1898
OIL ON CANVAS, 26.151
GIFT OF E. S. CLARK, F. A. CLARK,
R. S. CLARK, AND S. C. CLARK

Once, when Blum was at work in the old studios decorated by him with strutting peacocks, Oscar Wilde, then at the height of his celebrity, walked in and watched the progress of the artist. "Blum," he remarked, "your exquisite pastels give me the sensation of eating yellow satin." The brilliant esthete would have felt flattered had he known that the Japanese who saw Blum at work had experienced virtually the same original sensation.

MARTIN BIRNBAUM,
"ROBERT FREDERICK BLUM: AN APPRECIATION"

The Moral life of man forms part of the subject matter of the artist, but the morality of art consists in the perfect use of an imperfect medium.

OSCAR WILDE

Perhaps this view of what constitutes the good is natural and applicable in a culture which also holds that man was born in sin, whether in Biblical or in psychoanalytic terms. But should we , who believe that other cultures should be assessed according to their own categories and premises, impose upon them our own unexamined conception of the good and thus always see them as striving to remove or avoid ills? It seems to me that, when we do not take this negative view of the good for granted, other cultures often appear to be maintaining 'justment' rather than striving to attain adjustment.

KURT WOLFF,
"THIS IS THE TIME FOR RADICAL ANTHROPOLOGY"

LIST OF SOURCES

The history, and not just in terms: Michael Foucault, in Didier Eribon, *Michael Foucault* (Paris: Editions Flammarion, 1989), p. 118.

The savage lives within himself: Jean-Jacques Rousseau, "A Discourse on the Origin and Foundation of Inequality among Men" (1755), in Rousseau, *The Social Contract and Other Writings*, trans. G. D. H. Cole (London: J. M. Dent and Sons, 1941), p. 237.

M. Blair Coan, investigator: Milton Brown, *The Story of the Armory Show* (New York: Abbeville Press, 1988), p. 206.

"The body is the temple of God": Brown, *The Story of the Armory Show*, p. 206.

In a world of shifting values: Brown, *The Story of the Armory Show*, pp. 162–63.

Shortly before the arrival of the Show: Brown, *The Story of the Armory Show*, p. 205.

Their patterns of political: Ruth Benedict, *Race: Science and Politics* (New York: Viking, 1943), pp. 132–33.

In the formation of Muslim dogma: Sir Thomas W. Arnold, *Painting in Islam* (Oxford: Clarendon Press, 1928), pp. 6–7.

Sooner or later we shall have to: Edward Sapir, "Culture, Genuine and Spurious," in *Selected Writings of Edward Sapir in Language, Culture, and Personality*, David G. Mandelbaum, ed. (Berkeley: University of California Press, 1949), p. 331.

One should add that the natives' response: Stephen Greenblatt, "Filthy Rites," *Daedalus* 111 (Summer 1982), p. 3.

…when Malinowski ventured to suggest: Greenblatt, "Filthy Rites," p. 3.

145

The question returns: Leo Steinberg, *The Sexuality of Christ in Renaissance Art and in Modern Oblivion*, An October Book (New York: Pantheon, 1983), p. 180.

Granted that order spoils pattern: Mary Douglas, *Purity and Danger: An Analysis of Concepts of Pollution and Taboo* (London: Routledge & Kegan Paul, 1966), p. 94.

I found pictures at the exhibition: Maud J. Coan Josephare, quoted in Milton Brown, *The Story of the Armory Show*, p. 207.

Kendall and the artist Albert Herter: Robert Austin, "William Sergeant Kendall, Painter of Children," *Antiques* 124.5 (Nov. 1983), pp. 1028, 1027.

As soon as the photographic image is seen: David Freedberg, *The Power of Images* (Chicago: University of Chicago Press, 1989), p. 353.

Arousal by image (whether pornographic or not): Freedberg, *The Power of Images*, pp. 350–52.

From the pictures sent in for the exhibition: George L. Mosse, *Nazi Culture: Intellectual, Cultural, and Social Life in the Third Reich* (New York: Schocken, 1981), p. 15

The artist does not create for the artist: Hitler speaking at the opening of the House of German Art in Munich, July 18, 1937, in Mosse, *Nazi Culture*, p. 15.

The people when it passes through these galleries: Mosse, *Nazi Culture*, p. 16.

Office of the State Secret Police, Berlin: Hans M. Wingler, *Bauhaus*, ed. Joseph Stein, trans. Wolfgang Jabs and Basil Gilbert (Cambridge, Mass.: MIT Press, 1969), p. 189.

Behind the specific accusations which were made: Barbara Lane Miller, *Architecture and Politics in Germany, 1918 to 1945* (Cambridge, Mass., and London: Harvard University Press, 1968), p. 86.

No one must say that the people: Mosse, *Nazi Culture*, pp. 15–16.

The Exhibitions and publications of the Bauhaus: *Weimarische Zeitung* (July 6, 1929), quoted in Miller, *Architecture and Politics*, pp. 82–83.

Goebbels Forbids Art Criticism: Joseph Goebbels, quoted in Rolf Geissler, *Dekadenz und Heroismus* (Stuttgart: Deutsche Verlaganstalt, 1964), and translated in Mosse, *Nazi Culture*, pp. 162–63.

A few years ago, with this in mind: Dorothy Lee, "Are Basic Needs Ultimate?" in Lee, *Freedom and Culture* (Englewood Cliffs, N.J.: Prentice-Hall, 1959), pp. 53–54.

Assassination is the extreme form: George Bernard Shaw, quoted in Bartlett, *Familiar Quotations* (New York: Little, Brown, 1980), p. 681, no. 16

The people who assail images: Freedberg, *The Power of Images*, p. 418.

The mode of iconoclasm: Leo Steinberg, *The Sexuality of Christ*, p. 175.

Eakins' methods of instruction at the academy: Elizabeth Johns, *Thomas Eakins: The Heroism of Modern Life* (Princeton: Princeton University Press, 1983), pp. 109–10.

Carpenter (1971) reports in TV Guide: Sol Worth, "Toward an Anthropological Politics of Symbolic Form," in Hymes, ed., *Reinventing Anthropology*, p. 352. The parenthetical reference is to Edmund Carpenter, "Television Meets the Stone Age," *TV Guide* (Jan. 16, 1971), pp. 14–16.

When the makers of Pepsi Cola: Found newspaper clipping, source unknown.

If left unchecked, we and perhaps other nations: Sol Worth, "Toward an Anthropological Politics of Symbolic Form," in Hymes, ed., *Reinventing Anthropology*, p. 353.

The sanguine life and terrifying aspects: Stanley Diamond, "Primitive Society in Its Many Dimensions," in Kurt H. Wolff, Barrington Moore, Jr., et al., eds., *The Critical Spirit: Essays in Honor of Herbert Marcuse* (Boston: Beacon Press, 1967), p. 26.

To think deeply in our culture: Jules Henry, *Culture against Man* (New York: Random House: 1963), p. 146.

The moral life of man: Oscar Wilde, Preface to "The Picture of Dorian Gray," in *The Portable Oscar Wilde*, Richard Aldington, ed. (New York: Viking Press, 1946), p. 138.

Perhaps this view of what constitutes: Dorothy Lee, "Are Basic Needs Ultimate?" in Lee, *Freedom and Culture* (Englewood Cliffs, N.J.: Prentice-Hall, 1959), pp. 72–73.

Once, when Blum was at work: Martin Birnbaum, "Robert Frederick Blum: An Appreciation," in *Catalogue of a Memorial Loan Exhibition of the Works of Robert Frederick Blum* (New York: Berlin Photographic Co., 1913), pp. 9–10.

TYPOGRAPHY AND DESIGN
CHARLES NIX
WITH JOSEPH KOSUTH